I once heard a movie star mom share her exhilaration at adopting her infant son. When she saw him she announced, "Oh, *there* you are!" as if she'd been reconciled with a part of her own being. The hole of infertility is like that: tearing a part of our very being from ourselves. So very often we are left alone with our pain. Until now. Here, in the pages of *Mothers in Waiting*, you'll find a part of yourself reconnecting in the stories of others who've experienced this grief. Just like you...and just like me. And as you do, you'll likely hear an echo reverberating as you rediscover that lost part of your being, "Oh, *there* you are!"

—**Elisa Morgan**, Speaker,
author: *The Prayer Coin, The Beauty of Broken*
President Emerita MOPS International
Cohost, *Discover the Word*

"Who am I if I'm not a mother?" was the heart cry of Karen Granger, one of 30 women who bravely share their stories of hope in these beautiful pages, a question deeply reflecting their common sorrow. There was a season when my heart was so broken by our infertility struggles that I would not have been receptive to these diverse stories. Having admitted my struggle, I want to encourage you that if you are currently in a place of wanting to see a few of the many ways God can bring good from the grief and anguish of your barrenness while gathering a few hard-earned tips on how these women learned to find strength in Jesus through the midst of their pain, this is the book for you! When given to God, infertility always, eventually, leads to joyful resolution, often through some method of motherhood—birth, foster care, various forms of adoption, step—or sometimes by learning how to embrace God's unique, personal plan for your life as His daughter without children in your home. As Amanda Hope Haley points out in chapter 9, God's personal path for you dramatically differs from His unchangeable will for all mankind—to know Him. Infertility is sometimes the plan God allows us to journey to achieve His will in drawing our hearts to Himself. That path can be agonizing and seem unending while being endured. As these stories, each written from the "after" perspective of resolution, point out, the good plan God has for you is written in great love and will ultimately lead to your good and His glory.

—**Jennifer Saake**, Author of *Hannah's Hope*;
founder/director emeritus, Hannah's Prayer Ministries.
JenniferSaake.com

Mothers in Waiting

CRYSTAL BOWMAN & MEGHANN BOWMAN

HARVEST HOUSE PUBLISHERS
EUGENE, OREGON

Cover by Faceout Studio

Cover photo © united photo studio / Shutterstock

The authors are represented by the literary agency of Credo Communications, LLC, Grand Rapids, Michigan, www.credocommunications.net.

Mothers in Waiting
Copyright © 2019 Crystal Bowman and Meghann Bowman
Published by Harvest House Publishers
Eugene, Oregon 97408
www.harvesthousepublishers.com

ISBN 978-0-7369-7536-0 (pbk.)
ISBN 978-0-7369-7537-7 (eBook)

Library of Congress Cataloging-in-Publication Data

Names: Bowman, Crystal, author.
Title: Mothers in waiting / Crystal Bowman and Meghann Bowman.
Description: Eugene : Harvest House Publishers, 2018.
Identifiers: LCCN 2018028309 (print) | LCCN 2018044054 (ebook) | ISBN
    9780736975377 (ebook) | ISBN 9780736975360 (pbk.)
Subjects: LCSH: Christian women--Prayers and devotions. | Consolation. |
    Infertility--Religious aspects--Christianity.
Classification: LCC BV4527 (ebook) | LCC BV4527 .B68125 2018 (print) | DDC
    248.8/43--dc23
LC record available at https://lccn.loc.gov/2018028309

Printed in the United States of America
18 19 20 21 22 23 24 25 26 27 / BP-AR / 10 9 8 7 6 5 4 3 2 1

To our contributors—

Thank you for making our vision a reality
by sharing your courageous and heartfelt stories.

Contents

Glossary for Mothers in Waiting

IUI—intrauterine insemination: a procedure that involves placing sperm inside a woman's uterus to facilitate fertilization. By increasing the number of sperm that reach the fallopian tubes, it increases the chance of fertilization.

IVF—in vitro fertilization: a process that combines eggs and sperm outside the body in a laboratory. Once an embryo or embryos form, they are then placed in the uterus.

PCOS—polycystic ovarian syndrome: a hormone imbalance that can cause problems with a woman's ovaries, making it more difficult to conceive.

RE—reproductive endocrinologist: a fertility specialist who specializes in disorders of the female reproductive tract.

TTC—trying to conceive

You're Not Alone

Michael and Kathy met in college, fell in love, got married, and made the decision to start a family together. Month after month of negative pregnancy tests turned into an unexpected journey of rigid schedules, invasive testing, expensive medical procedures, countless tears, and lost hope.

Does this sound familiar? According to the Centers for Disease Control and Prevention, about 10 percent of women in the United States ages 15-44 have difficulty getting pregnant or staying pregnant. That's about 6.1 million women whose bodies work a little differently when it comes to having a baby. When infertility rules your life, the downward emotional spiral begins. Everyday experiences become painful reminders. A trip to the grocery store can bring you to tears as your eyes turn toward women with swollen bellies or mothers with toddlers strapped in shopping carts. You stay home from church on Mother's Day, and you cringe when you receive another baby shower invitation. It also takes a toll on your marriage as making love turns into making babies.

It's not that you aren't happy for other women who have babies; it's just that your heart hurts, and your empty arms ache. Probably the worst thing is hearing thoughtless comments from friends and family who should know better—"When are you guys going to have kids?" "How long have you been married? And no kids yet?" "I want to be a grandma. What's taking so long?"—and then you hear stories of teen pregnancies, abortions, and neglected children that make your blood boil. You just want to be a mom, and you know you'd be a good one.

If, sadly, the word *infertile* describes you, then you are a member of a club you didn't want to be in. It can be a lonely journey with little emotional support. It's a subject many don't want to talk about. That's why we created this book. Every woman who has experienced infertility has a story to tell, and every story is unique. This book shares the stories of 30 different women who have walked this road and who are here to come alongside you on your journey.

These stories are not just about women. They are also stories of husbands and families and children. They are stories of loss and redemption, of miracle babies and adopted children who will grow up to find God's purpose for their lives.

God puts children in our lives in a variety of ways. While only God knows how your story will be written, our hope is that these offerings will bring you comfort. And our prayer is that you will find peace in knowing that God cares about you and your family, and He sees the desires of your heart—whether that heart is grieving, celebrating, or waiting on Him.

1

Those Who Sow Tears

Katherine Alumbaugh

MY STORY

When my husband and I got married, we often spoke of how much we looked forward to being parents. After meeting online and dating long-distance, we got married almost one year to the day from when we met in person for the first time. We decided to adjust to married life for our first year before trying to get pregnant. But we knew we wanted a big family, so we didn't want to wait too long.

I had a "pre-pregnancy" appointment with my ob-gyn as our first anniversary drew close. I had carefully tracked my cycles as part of our natural family planning method of birth control. The doctor said everything looked great, and "it should only take you a few months to get pregnant since you've been tracking everything so well." We booked an anniversary trip to New Zealand and hoped we'd come home to find out we were pregnant.

But we didn't. The next month was the same. And the next. Month after month ticked by with negative pregnancy tests. In the midst of that season, my husband received a job offer in Texas, so we moved across the country. I kept telling myself, *It's from the stress of moving.* So we kept waiting.

When I don't understand something, my first reaction is to study it. I searched for answers, amazed at how God designed this miracle of life to work. But I couldn't figure out why it wasn't working for us. The knowledge made me crazy. I can't even remember how many times I thought I was pregnant. Did I just feel implantation cramping? Was that a wave of nausea? We rode the same roller coaster each month.

After ten months of trying, I scheduled a visit at my new ob-gyn office. The nurse practitioner agreed it was time to do a few more tests. My blood work came back great, and secondary tests also revealed nothing. As we drew closer to our second anniversary and one year of trying to conceive, we decided to make an appointment with a fertility specialist.

In the midst of this journey, we had also discussed adoption and attended a conference to learn more about the process and realities of adoption. While we were open to adoption, we also wanted to have biological children. Both paths can be expensive, time-consuming, and heart-wrenching. We decided to pursue fertility treatment first because, at 30 years old, I was still relatively young.

The following year was consumed by doctor's appointments, blood draws, and various procedures. Since we had the frustrating diagnosis of "unexplained infertility," we started with a conservative approach for several months. Every pregnancy test came back negative. Our next step was exploratory surgery, but, alas, no answers. We added acupuncture. I adjusted my diet and took additional supplements. Still, every pregnancy test came back negative.

That fall, our doctor recommended we move on to in vitro fertilization (IVF) because, statistically, if the previous treatments were going to work, they would have by that point. I was physically, emotionally, and spiritually exhausted. I had been poked, prodded, and cut into. We were desperate for answers, but ultimately we just wanted a baby.

After studying and praying, we decided to move forward with IVF. The night we started the IVF medication, my hands shook as I tried to fill the syringe with the precisely prescribed amount of extremely expensive medication. I started sobbing, and my husband stepped in to help me and finish giving me the shot. The first shot was the hardest. Eventually, we got the hang of it.

All of the infertility treatments we went through felt invasive and, in some aspects, humiliating. The egg retrieval and embryo transfers were the worst. I felt completely exposed in every possible way.

Our egg retrieval went smoothly, and we ended up with three embryos. Due to frustrating scheduling conflicts, we had to wait eight weeks before we could transfer one embryo. We meticulously followed the protocol and prayed like crazy. Nine days later, we found out the embryo hadn't implanted. Our hearts broke.

We decided to take a break for a few months. We felt beat up in every way. My body felt like it didn't belong to me anymore. Since we never discovered the reason for our infertility, we used that time to check out anything else that could be going on with my health before we transferred another embryo.

I felt so frustrated over those few months. I saw a number of other doctors, but no one had any answers. Eventually, we decided it was time to transfer another embryo. One hot July day, we woke up early, nervous and excited. A few hours later, we saw a tiny embryo on an ultrasound picture as the doctor performed the transfer. Smaller than a poppy seed, those few cells were our daughter. That experience brought a new and deeper understanding of the phrase "fearfully and wonderfully made."

MY STRUGGLE

In my early twenties, one of my greatest fears became a reality. I lost my dad unexpectedly. We had had a difficult relationship, and our last conversation ended in an argument. A few months after his passing, the Lord led me to seminary. Through counseling and godly friends, I found a safe place to grieve. But in the classroom I wrestled with theology. I had to ask questions about God's sovereignty. As far as I know, my dad did not know Christ. And that haunted me. It forced me to ask the really hard questions: Was God real? How could He allow so much suffering? Was He truly good? How could the Lord, who says He loves me and my dad, allow him to die after I had spent years praying for his salvation and for the restoration of our relationship before either happened? How could God leave me with no answers?

There isn't space to do justice to how the Lord led me through that process. But He ultimately brought me peace. Was God really there? *Yes, He was.* Is He really good? *Yes, He is good.*

When we were facing infertility, it became apparent that God was allowing another fear to come true: I might never be a mother. I didn't struggle with the same questions this time. I had a deep certainty that God was real and that He was good. But there were times when I just didn't know where He was. It felt like He was ignoring us and was deaf to our crying.

My theology training told me those things couldn't be true. God can't be anything other than who He is. And He is always loving, and He is always present with those who have placed their faith in Him. But there were many days when I didn't feel it. I felt overwhelmed by the heartache of wanting a child. I yearned to see my husband as a dad, and I was frustrated to have my infertility "unexplained."

MY STRENGTH

In His great kindness, the Lord prepared me ahead of time—even before I met my husband—to walk through those infertility years. My mentor during seminary was one of the few female professors on campus. We had similar academic interests, so I happily took a number of her classes, interned with her, and wrote my thesis under her supervision. Over time, I learned that she and her husband had faced years of infertility and suffered miscarriage after miscarriage. Ultimately, they adopted a beautiful baby girl, who was a teenager when I met her.

My professor wrote a number of books on infertility, but more than that, she shared how infertility had shaken her to her core. She questioned what it meant to be a Christian woman. Then in Scripture she found that the highest calling of a woman is not to be a wife and mother; it's to be a follower of Christ.

When faced with my own infertility journey, I didn't have to question my womanhood. As desperately as I wanted children, I knew motherhood was not God's highest calling on my life. I also knew that God builds families in surprising and miraculous ways. And from my own experience of grief, I knew that God can bring beauty and healing from ashes.

> The highest calling of a woman is not to be a
> wife and mother; it's to be a follower of Christ.

I wish this weren't true about me, but I've found I draw closest to the Lord during times of great suffering. When life feels smooth, I get distracted. But when my heart aches, I know from experience that true relief only comes from the Lord. I know He won't always give me specific answers. But He is always there with me.

MY SCRIPTURE

> *Those who sow in tears*
> *Shall reap in joy.*
> *He who continually goes forth weeping,*
> *Bearing seed for sowing,*
> *Shall doubtless come again with rejoicing,*
> *Bringing his sheaves with him (Psalm 126:5-6).*

I haven't had many experiences when I've felt the Lord direct me specifically to a verse. But after walking through infertility for a while, my husband and I decided to read through the Bible together in a year. On one particularly difficult day, I read this verse. The words jumped off the page! They reminded me that God is the God of *life*. Death and barrenness and infertility are not from Him. They are side effects of living in a fallen, broken world. God is the God of *joy* and *life*. So much so that He sent His Son to save our world from all its brokenness. No matter what, joy is ultimately coming.

A few days later, I found the same verse quoted in a book. It felt like a physical weight on my chest. When I had read the verses a few days before, they had reminded me of theological truths that brought me comfort. But unexpectedly seeing the same verse again felt like God was gently taking my face in His hands so I would hear His words. My husband and I had been sowing in tears for so long. We had been weeping while planting seeds of hope with every cycle, every procedure, every test. By this point, I felt confident that God would build our family one way or another. But these verses reminded me that *joy* was waiting for us specifically. Our tears would not go on forever. We would hold our child in our arms one day.

2

Plans for Good

Meghann Bowman

MY STORY

When I was in college, I had extremely irregular and painful periods that lasted from seven to ten days and that came and went with no pattern. The "solution" prescribed by the various doctors I saw was the birth control pill. The pill did regulate my cycle, and because everyone I knew also took the pill, I never thought about the negatives associated with its use.

Fast-forward eight years—to the year of my engagement to my now-husband—when I decided that I would go off the pill in order to lose a few vanity pounds for my upcoming nuptials. My period did not return after eight months. I saw multiple gynecologists during this time, all of whom were quick to insist that I go back on the pill to regain my cycle because there are many negative health risks associated with not menstruating. While I had a nagging feeling that something wasn't quite right, I listened to their advice and attributed the lack of periods to stress, anxiety, and weight loss.

Two years after my husband and I were married, I stopped taking the pill again with the intent to regain my cycle so that when we were ready to get pregnant, I would be able to conceive. I waited and waited for my period to return, but after eight months, it still did not. Against the advice of my gynecologist, I was determined to fix it without taking birth control pills. Over the course of the next three years, I started eating lots of carbs and little fat, then ate no carbs and lots of fat. I exercised less, then exercised more. I took herbs and supplements and did acupuncture. On the advice of a naturopath, I removed gluten, dairy, and sugar from my diet to cure my "adrenal fatigue." None of these things induced a period. My gynecologist also tried to induce a period medically with Provera, which also did nothing. At this point, I had to admit to myself that there was something more serious going on, and we moved on to seeing a reproductive endocrinologist (RE).

We began seeing an RE recommended to us by a friend of a friend who swore this one was "the best." After working with him for six months, I had no diagnosis and more questions than answers. We also realized that the medications I was being prescribed were not producing the desired response. I moved on to a second RE, who did more extensive testing and diagnosed me with hypothalamic amenorrhea. To me, this was a diagnosis for elite marathon runners and Olympic gymnasts, not an average-weight, average-pace jogger me. I again tried to take my health into my own hands (changed my diet, changed my exercise habits, saw a therapist, did acupuncture) while simultaneously doing intrauterine insemination (IUI) cycles. I only had one instance where the actual IUI procedure was done because while my ovarian reserve was good, the doctor could not seem to elicit a response from my "sleeping" ovaries with various medications in small or large doses. At this point, the only option left on the table was IVF.

My husband is not into waiting. If there is a problem, he wants a solution immediately and will find a solution no matter the cost. He was very adamant that we were not getting the care we needed and wanted to try one of the big-name clinics for IVF. I was more resistant because I did not want to be inconvenienced by the travel, logistics, and costs associated with a long-distance clinic. After much prayer and heartache, we decided that we did not want to waste any more time, and we began the IVF process with a clinic 2,000 miles away from us.

The process was all of the things that I feared, but I also realized the doctors were much more capable than those we had seen previously, and I had peace about our decision to be there. They were able to precisely identify the right medications in the right doses, and I produced a large number of eggs. While I did have to freeze everything because my estrogen level rose too high for a fresh transfer, the embryos seemed to be of good quality, and we were hopeful. However, hope turned to heartbreak when I miscarried a few weeks after my first frozen transfer. I was devastated. If the very best embryo didn't work, how did we have a chance with any of the others?

I busied myself with work and with life, not wanting to deal with the roller coaster of emotions. I shut out my husband, never considering his hurt in this process. In my mind, it was all about me. I was a failure as a wife if I could not bear children. We geared up for another frozen transfer toward the end of the year, but my heart was not into it. I kept at it because the timing was convenient, and our insurance deductible had been satisfied for the year.

Once we were at the clinic, though, I couldn't go through with the procedure. My heart could not handle any more loss, and I needed an indefinite break. I stopped taking all of the medication I was on and mentally gave up my fight. We flew home with heavy hearts and uncertainty in our marriage.

> I busied myself with work and with life, not wanting to deal with the roller coaster of emotions.

God had other plans, though, and eight weeks later I learned I was pregnant. Naturally. With no intervention. I had not ovulated in at least ten years, so obviously—I concluded—the pregnancy test was wrong. I took six more tests, then scoured the internet for all the reasons for a false positive. But, nine months later, I gave birth to a six-pound, eight-ounce healthy miracle. When I failed to regain my cycle after pregnancy, I was told by my doctor that I shouldn't expect to get pregnant again, so we treated our son as if he would be our one and only. Again, God's plans differed, and as I write this, I am midway through my second trimester with an apparently healthy baby girl.

God has revealed Himself to us in immeasurable ways through parenthood. The concepts of unconditional love and grace were foreign to us before this experience. Our God is with us and for us, in good times and in bad. God did not forsake me during my fertility struggle, but more importantly, I realized that God would never have forsaken me even if He had not opened the door to my being a mother because I am His daughter.

MY STRUGGLE

Throughout my life, hard work and determination led to achievement. The reality that fertility was out of my control was challenging, to say the least. I worked and exercised obsessively to cope, and I retreated from close relationships, especially my relationship with my husband. I was ashamed of my infertility and envious of the fertility of those around me. I didn't want anyone to see my hurt, so I attended every baby shower I was invited to and served in a ministry at church where I prepared and delivered meals to families with new babies. My Achilles heel was baby baptisms. Our pastor always quoted Psalm 127:3, which says that "children are a gift from the LORD; they are a reward from him" (NLT). When would I get my reward? Was I being punished by God? I now know that God doesn't work like this and that the word *reward* is actually more synonymous with *gift*, something for which we did nothing. There is nothing we can do to earn God's favor. The only thing we contribute to our salvation is our sin.

MY STRENGTH

I found solace in connecting with others who were struggling with infertility. Hearing their stories was comforting—not because I thought their outcomes would be the same as mine, but because I realized I was not alone. I read the blogs of people I will never meet, cried with one of my closest friends from college, and attended RESOLVE group support meetings. These connections sustained me through my journey because they eased the feeling of loneliness.

MY SCRIPTURE

I know the plans I have for you,
declares the LORD, *plans for welfare and not for evil,*
to give you a future and a hope (Jeremiah 29:11 ESV).

This verse hangs on my son's wall because I want him to know that God has a plan for him, but really this verse has so much meaning to me. While struggling with infertility, I was reminded and comforted by the fact that God wants what is *good* for us. God's will is not always our will. Upon the arrival of my precious baby, I was overcome with the feeling that he was *meant* for me. The timing of his birth was all in God's plan. My waiting had nothing to do with me; I was merely a chapter in God's story of my baby's life.

3

Reap in Joy

Jillian Burden

MY STORY

I counted backward to the day: forty weeks from my seminary graduation. That's when my husband, John, and I would try to conceive. I could not wait one day longer. I imagined myself waddling down the graduation aisle, a swollen belly protruding beneath my gown. My body *hungered* for pregnancy. I could feel the kicks and rolls of a phantom baby inside me long before we were ready to try.

We were active and healthy, John and I. We ate whole grains and greens. My cycles were regular. I read books about conception and charted my basal body temperature. It would take three months to conceive. Probably fewer. My heart quickened at the thought of it! We were ready.

When only one line showed up on our first pregnancy test, I thought I tested too early. My bleeding followed shortly, however, and I knew it hadn't been our month. Disappointed but not deterred, we tried again. We were discouraged when the second month yielded another negative test, but we tried again. Again, nothing. It was early in our journey, but after a third month passed with no pregnancy, I knew something was wrong. I could feel it.

As the months passed, the size of the belly I had pictured under my graduation gown grew smaller and smaller until it was a tiny bump, then a secret only I would know, and then...nothing at all. At my graduation

I was simultaneously filled with the satisfaction of my degree and hollowed out by nine months of fruitless trying.

As John and I approached the one-year mark, we knew we were heading toward an official diagnosis of infertility. Why was this happening to us? I longed for answers both medical and spiritual.

We met with a doctor at our local fertility center, and we also began conversations with a few adoption agencies. Through a journey of prayer and counsel from both friends and professionals, we decided to adopt before pursuing fertility treatment.

More than a year later, we brought a beautiful, cheerful, tender two-and-a-half-year-old boy home from Russia. We met him on a rainy day in his Moscow orphanage. After months of memorizing his every feature from pictures, I was astonished by his beautiful bodily presence before me. A mother will kiss her baby after birth, tears mixing with the vernix and blood on her newborn's skin, and I wanted to kiss the child before me. I wanted to breathe him in and look over every inch of his perfect body. *He was beautiful! He was mine!*

He was a toddler, though, not a newborn, and I was yet a stranger. Reining in my unbridled heart, I spoke softly to him and gently touched his hands, his back, the dark hair on his head. It didn't matter that he hadn't come from my body. He was mine. I was in love. I was a mother.

After our son had been home for a year, we were ready to make him a big brother. John and I went back to our fertility clinic. I underwent blood work, diagnostic procedures, medicated cycles, four intrauterine inseminations, and one surgery. We came away from a full year of tests and treatment with a diagnosis of diminished ovarian reserve and endometriosis.

Our doctor explained the only option left for us was IVF. But I had previously heard about embryo adoption, which is essentially doing IVF with donated embryos. That seemed like a great fit for us! The term *embryo adoption* is a bit of a misnomer because there is no legal adoption involved due to the way embryos are viewed legally in the USA. Whether we use the term *embryo adoption* or *donor embryo IVF*, this choice meant that we would be conceiving with embryos another couple had created during their own struggle with infertility and were unable to use.

We connected with an amazing couple who decided to donate four embryos to us, and so began our journey into embryo adoption. Feeling renewed hope, we transferred two embryos on our first cycle. We waited two weeks. I had my blood drawn. A nurse called me with the results: not pregnant. We spent that Christmas grieving. I hung two snowflake ornaments on my tree in memory of the embryos we had lost.

In the new year we tried again with our remaining embryos. We waited two weeks. I had my blood drawn. A nurse called us with the news we had been waiting years to hear: I was pregnant! We spent the next month both rejoicing and anxiously waiting for our first ultrasound. We could not wait to see our tiny baby, or two tiny babies!

When the time for our ultrasound arrived, I lay back on the patient bed. Our cheerful doctor smiled and said, "Let's take a look!" The ultrasound began, and within seconds it was obvious that something was wrong. Where our baby should have been, there was nothing. My world went silent except for a ringing in my ears. Our baby had stopped growing, and I was going to miscarry.

When I did miscarry, I felt as though I was dying with my baby. As I fought to survive my grief, I realized the pain of our loss had somehow intensified my hunger for pregnancy. I wondered if I was crazy to want to try again. I fought to suppress my desire, to be content with the life I already had, to picture a future in which I never saw my belly grow, never experienced the pangs of birth, never felt a baby slip from my womb into the world, never lived that dream. I could not. I had to try again.

With no remaining embryos, John and I put our names on a list at our clinic's anonymous embryo donation program. We were matched with a set of embryos, and we prepared my body for a third transfer. We transferred two embryos. We waited two weeks. I had my blood drawn. A nurse called with the news: I was pregnant. Our joy was tempered by anxiety. Our hearts and minds were set on that first ultrasound. Would a baby (or babies) be there, growing and alive?

As I fought to survive my grief, I realized
the pain of our loss had somehow
intensified my hunger for pregnancy.

The day arrived. Driving to our ultrasound I shook so hard with fear that my teeth chattered. A new doctor came into the office, and as I lay back on that same patient bed, she moved her ultrasound wand to reveal not just one, but two beautiful, tiny babies.

My belly grew all fall and winter. I experienced pregnancy in its fullness—the joy, the growth, the nausea, the kicks and rolls, the aches and pains, and the miraculous feeling of new life inside. One April night, waters splashed from my body, my belly tightened with ever-increasing pain, and I pushed two perfect baby boys into the world. Years of longing, fulfilled.

MY STRUGGLE

A believer from childhood, I had been taught that my faith would not keep me from trials. But what I discovered during my journey to motherhood was that I believed my faith would keep me from pain. I believed God would lead me through trials with a comfort that protected me from the depth of grief that came with those trials. I thought of the martyrs who were burned at the stake and died singing, seeming to be carried above the torturous pain of the flames. I thought, if subconsciously, that my faith would buoy my spirit so that I would never go fully under the waters of grief.

Infertility took a toll on my body but, more so, on my spirit. The faith I had carried as a child into early adulthood was deconstructed as I realized that God was not going to keep me away from pain. He was not going to protect me from losing my baby nor the crushing grief that came with it.

Who was this God I served? He was different from the God I thought I knew.

MY STRENGTH

I am still reconstructing my faith after infertility. I believe the journey tore down parts of my faith that were not true, so I would be open to knowing God more truly and experiencing His gifts more fully.

I have learned that, in His wisdom, God allows His children to both face trials and to experience the full depth of pain and grief that come with them. We cannot know the many trials from which He *has* protected us, yet He does allow some to pass by His sovereign hand.

So in these trials, where is God? I believe God is in the many gifts we discover in the midst of our trials. I saw God in the tender affection shown to me by His people during our season of infertility. He was in the encouraging texts from friends, the warm meals brought to our door, and the tokens of memory offered after our miscarriage. I saw God in the incredible gifting of His servants—the social workers, the nannies at the orphanage, the nurses, the doctors who worked passionately to bring our son home from Russia and to give life to our twins. Most clearly, I saw God in the inexplicable strength I found to persevere through years of infertility treatments and loss. When I questioned if I was crazy to submit myself to another procedure, take another pill, inject another shot, spend more money on medical expenses, risk the pain of another loss, God's Spirit was strong in me. He was the small voice telling me not to give up yet. His mighty hand upheld me as I persevered. In my weakness He was strong.

MY SCRIPTURE

> *Those who sow in tears*
> *Shall reap in joy (Psalm 126:5).*

This is the Scripture passage I carried on my infertility journey. It has two meanings to me. First, I sowed with tears throughout my journey to motherhood, and since then I have reaped the joy of my three children. Every single tear I wept on the journey toward them was worth it. Second, since my life is not over, neither are my trials. Now that my eyes are opened to the great suffering in our world, I often sow with tears. I sow acts of love and compassion while I weep over the suffering of humankind. But I do so with hope because I know I will one day—when Christ returns to make all things new—celebrate with songs of joy. As I have persevered through many trials to build my family, I have my eyes set on my future with the family of God where we will together sing our eternal song of joy.

4

Desires of Your Heart

Valorie Burton

MY STORY

I love being around family. It's where I've always felt joy, freedom, and contentment. Growing up in an Air Force family, I nevertheless spent many childhood summers in my parents' hometown in South Carolina. By the time I was ten, I had lived in Florida, Germany, and Colorado—far away from extended family. I went to college in Colorado and California before transferring and graduating from Florida State University. I earned a master's degree in journalism from Florida A&M University and enjoyed my twenties as a single professional woman. I was marketing director for an accounting firm in Dallas before starting my own marketing and public relations firm there. At age 26, I published my first book, and a couple years later, I sold my business to pursue my passion and calling: inspiring others to live more fulfilling lives.

I married when I was 30 and moved to Maryland, just outside Washington, DC, I continued writing books and speaking, then went back to graduate school and earned a master's degree in applied positive psychology from the University of Pennsylvania. I had always wanted to have children, but my then-spouse and I were not on the same page. When the marriage ended after six years, I was thankful we did not have children.

After my divorce, I spent a few months in South Carolina to be with family, then moved to Atlanta to start a new life. With nearly 20 relatives in Atlanta, I felt it would be a soft spot to land during a very difficult time in my life. I was 36 and divorced, yet I still held out hope that a happy marriage and family were a possibility for me.

A little over three years after moving to Atlanta, a classmate from high school saw one of my books in an airport and tagged me in a post on Facebook. I met Jeff for lunch, and it soon became obvious we were meant for each other. A little over a year later, we married. Besides marrying a wonderful man, I was also blessed with two sweet, beautiful, energetic bonus daughters (our replacement word for *step*) who were six and nine when we became a family.

We wanted to have a child together, and after about six months of trying, we went to an infertility doctor. I was 41. I was encouraged by all of the various tests. During one of the tests, a doctor even proclaimed I had a "textbook uterus"! The process was tiring, but I believed we would conceive. My mom had a baby at 41, and my grandmother had her last child at 40. Although I was told getting pregnant after 40 was not genetically likely, I was encouraged by my family history.

The IVF procedure was emotionally draining with many ups and downs. I never would have thought I could give myself shots multiple times per day. But I wanted a child, and the sacrifice of shots and tests and the daily trips to the doctor were worth it to me. I decided that I would give this one try—one round of IVF treatment—and if it didn't work, I would not try again. I knew that if I did not try at all, I would always wonder, *What if?* We had two healthy embryos implanted, and I was soon pregnant with twins! We shared our good news with family and were full of hope and anticipation.

When I miscarried at seven-and-a half weeks, we were devastated. The thought of losing our babies had never entered our minds. Telling the girls brought another layer of sadness. When we broke the news, they both collapsed in my lap and sobbed for nearly 30 minutes. When they gathered themselves, they both said the sweetest things. Addie, my youngest bonus daughter, said, "We will see them again one day when we get to heaven." And Sophie, then ten years old, spoke with hope: "There are a lot of children who need a home. Maybe we can adopt a baby." The girls did not know that Jeff and I had already planned to adopt, even if we gave birth to children because we had never shared that with them.

After the miscarriage, I gave myself time to process what had happened. I grappled with the idea of never giving birth. I didn't try to make sense of it. I did not understand, but I made a conscious decision to trust God. I believed wholeheartedly that if I were meant to have a child, I would. And if I were not meant to have a child, I must accept that and embrace the many gifts my life offers me.

A couple months later, I was talking to a friend about my journey and mentioned that we were thinking about adoption. She said to me, "What are you waiting for? You're 42. You have a wonderful husband who is supportive, a home and community that would be wonderful for any child, bonus daughters who want another sibling."

The next week another friend asked the same question. Their questions resonated so deeply. *What was I waiting for?* Now was the time. I called a friend who'd adopted two boys and had previously encouraged me to reach out to the adoption consultant she and her husband worked with.

She said to me, "What are you waiting for?"

I called her, and just two weeks later, Jeff and I met with an adoption consultant who works with multiple agencies around the country. We were overwhelmed by the daunting amount of paperwork, but we decided to dig in and get it done. We completed all of the forms, background checks, medical tests, social worker visits, and more in less than a month. Everyone we met during the process said it would be quick. We were surprised and delighted, but a little apprehensive about believing it could happen quickly. But in June of 2015, two months and one day after our first meeting with the adoption consultant, our son was in our arms!

Alex arrived in our lives already a year old, energetic, and with a smile that makes you want to cuddle and kiss him again and again. In the first two minutes we held our son—we were still sitting in the adoption agency—my husband looked into Alex's big brown eyes and said, "I'm your daddy."

Without missing a beat, Alex looked up and said, "Dada!" and then fell into Jeff's lap giggling. It was an astonishing moment, a moment followed by so many others that confirmed for us the miracle of our immediate bond as a family. We were told it could take a few weeks for Alex to bond with us, but the bond was instant. That night as he splashed and laughed in the bathtub, he looked up at me as if to say, "Oh, good! You finally showed up!"

My journey to motherhood lasted more than a decade and was a path filled with disappointment and anguish, surrender and hope. Of all the babies on the planet, the Lord orchestrated events and people and circumstances in such a way that the baby who was destined to be ours entered our lives as though he'd been waiting for us all along.

MY STRUGGLE

When my first marriage ended, the enemy whispered doubts and lies into my ear. He tried to make me believe my life was over and I wouldn't be able to bounce back from this experience. It took a lot of strength to push through. I had lost six years of my life, and I would never get them back. I began to doubt that I would find the kind of love I believed in. Starting over in my late thirties also made me wonder if my dream of having children would ever come true. I love children and had always looked forward to the day when I would have some of my own. I worried that I would never get to experience motherhood because it would soon be too late.

As a newly divorced woman, I was also concerned that churches wouldn't invite me to speak. I felt I no longer had the right to write books or inspire others. These were lies the enemy wanted me to believe. But rather than believe those lies, I started talking back to them: "God still has a purpose for my life even though it may not be turning out the way I had planned. I'm choosing to be grateful for my life, and I will make the most of it. I am resilient! It's in my blood!" Talking back to the enemy's lies allowed me to change my focus. I chose to believe God could give us children, and if I didn't have children, then I knew God had other—better—plans. If some churches didn't invite me to speak, others would. Writing is my divinely inspired mission, and I have the right to write. The enemy would love for me to stop living my purpose, and I didn't want to give him that satisfaction. Fighting the enemy is hard, but we do not fight alone.

MY STRENGTH

The fear following my divorce weighed heavily on my shoulders until one day I looked it straight in the face! I sat in bed, praying and meditating, when a transformational message emerged from my doubt. I asked myself, "What if you never marry?" and "What if you never have a child?" I pictured my life 10, 20, even 50 years into the future. Then I began to answer those questions. Here's what I realized: The world would not come to an end, so I'd better learn to be happy regardless of the outcome! If I didn't get married or have children, I would live my life single without children and would choose to have an incredible life. There are many women I greatly admire who are single without children. They're happy, purposeful, loved, and loving. Furthermore, I already had children in my life whom I could love and influence if I never had my own. I thought about God's will for my life. His perfect will was what I wanted—and still want. Soon the burden lifted. My fear turned to hopeful thoughts: "You have a good life. You have time. With God, all things are possible. You will be free of the burden of fear and uncertainty if you let go of the need to understand it all."

When I chose to embrace *what is* rather than dwelling on *what if,* my faith for the future became stronger. Accepting that I might not get what I wanted allowed me to believe in my dream without holding it so tightly that I crushed it. In the midst of a storm, we can find it hard to believe anything good will come, but it will. Sometimes it takes years to see what God is doing in a difficult situation, but when we live with patience and faith, the good becomes more obvious. Choosing to believe that God is orchestrating the final outcome for our good can provide the motivation we need to persevere in the face of overwhelming odds.

When I chose to embrace *what is,*
rather than dwelling on *what if,* my faith
for the future became stronger.

Having children was a dream deferred, but I never gave up on the vision of marriage and family I had sensed deep in my spirit. At times, I felt frustrated, helpless, and discouraged, but I refused to give up hope. I could not. To give up hope would be to give up on God. So my advice to others is to keep hoping. Without hope, there is no vision. When you stop hoping, you start settling. Keep believing in your vision and make decisions that honor your ultimate goal. Keep a gratitude journal. Write about things that you are grateful for, and ask God to show you His message in your circumstances. Know that what you are going through is challenging, but the choice of how to respond is up to you. If God is the source of your stability, you will have strength to make it through.

MY SCRIPTURE

Delight yourself in the Lord,
*and he will give you the desires of
your heart (Psalm 37:4* esv).

One morning before my divorce, I sat alone in church trying to make sense of my desire to have children. I raised my hands to the Lord and asked Him to take away this desire if that was not His will. I wanted peace. I wanted to be happy for other women who were having children. I told God, "I will give up having kids if that is what You want."

After church I saw a woman whom I needed to talk to about something totally unrelated. She was an acquaintance. Not someone who knew me well. But when she saw me, her eyes widened as she told me about a dream she had had that morning before she woke up. "I dreamed you had a little girl who looked just like you." She placed her hands on my stomach and asked if I was pregnant. This dream really affected her, though she had no idea what was going on in my personal life.

I went to my car and cried out to God, "Clearly, You aren't telling me I'm not supposed to be a mother!" I realized I was trying to suppress and ignore what I wanted. I also realized that I felt guilty about wanting to have children. Then God's word came to me clearly: *I placed that desire in you, and I am not taking it away.*

The biggest lesson I've learned from my journey to motherhood is this: Hold on to the vision God has placed in your heart, but let go of your ideas about how it must come together. His plan will be even more beautiful than the one you imagined.

5

Keep Your Heart with All Diligence

Karen DeVries

MY STORY

After finishing a second round of college education to begin a new career, I was eager to start a family. I had walked away from a sales and marketing position to become an elementary school teacher because I imagined myself as a working mom while raising my four children. (If my "two girls and two boys" formula didn't pan out, I could be flexible about the genders and let God decide.) Teaching would allow me to work without travel demands, be home earlier each day, and share time off during the summers. It was a well-thought-out plan.

We began to pursue pregnancy when I was student teaching. Many times my periods would be about two weeks late, but I was never officially pregnant. My doctor said these were mini-miscarriages, but what did that mean? Was I pregnant and experiencing the loss of babies—or not?

We were referred to an infertility clinic, and the initial visit left us overwhelmed. We didn't want drugs, injections, temperature charts, or emotional and ethical discussions. We just wanted to be parents. After two frustrating years of experimenting with different medications, we were finally pregnant! Overjoyed, we called everyone to share the wonderful news. Our family plan was in motion!

A few weeks later I woke up during the night to a warm, wet feeling and a knowing dread. The doctor told us to head to the hospital for tests, and I was soon taken into a room for a D&C. After the procedure, a nurse said she didn't know why it was ordered because she didn't see any evidence of a pregnancy. The doctor later confirmed that I had indeed been in the early stages of pregnancy.

At that point, the emotional and financial cost of moving into the next steps was too much to consider. Calling everyone to share our devastating news brought back the tears we thought we could leave behind. We decided to stop trying to get pregnant. We couldn't imagine continuing the cycle of trying, then waiting, only to end in crying.

The families at my school came in many forms: blended, combinations of adopted and biological children, all adopted children, all biological children. It didn't matter: A family is a family regardless of how the children came into a couple's life.

One day a volunteer mom asked when my husband and I were going to have kids. I had been private about our journey of heartbreak, but her directness opened an emotional door for me, and I told her everything. She asked if we had considered adoption. I told her we had information about an attorney in town who specialized in adoption, but we weren't ready to make the call.

Six months later, the volunteer mom called with a shocking gift—the telephone number of a pregnant birth mother who was looking for a couple like us. Our hope returned. It was after 10:00 p.m., but we called the attorney that night, and the process of adopting our baby boy began. We knew from the moment he was placed into our arms that God had handpicked our son. My husband, Dale, and I were ready to begin our new life as parents.

When our son was two years old, the yearning for a sibling whispered. My two-girl-two-boy idea was long gone because I was learning to accept God's sovereign plan. He had let us become parents by way of adoption. How could we test Him? Besides, wasn't it selfish to want more, to want another miracle, this time a pregnancy? Did wanting more diminish our blessings? I tried to dodge my inner analytics because—as a woman of childbearing age who couldn't do the one basic thing that she was biologically supposed to do—I had lost a lot of self-confidence. We had our baby, so I hushed the whisper of hope for another baby each time it pressed.

Another turn of events came in the form of unbearable monthly cramps, which led to laparoscopic surgery to remove endometriosis. The doctor explained that after surgery I would be very fertile, but with each monthly cycle, the chance of pregnancy would fade. He suggested a six-month window to try to conceive; we agreed to three.

With drug therapy, artificial insemination, and progesterone injections, I was able to become pregnant and maintain a healthy pregnancy. I woke up before dawn one January morning, and this time the warm, wet feeling brought a knowing joy: My water broke! I made it to 40 weeks, just a few days shy of my due date. We risked driving to the hospital through a Michigan ice storm to welcome our second miracle baby.

We were happy and blessed with two beautiful children. This was God's perfect plan for our family. And when our firstborn was six years old, I realized that God had a greater purpose for our adoption experience. Our son needed a kidney transplant, and I was a match. Even though I didn't give birth to him, God allowed me to give him life by donating a kidney.

MY STRUGGLE

Being a private person, I found it hard to share my experiences with others. I carefully confided in the important women in my life. I shared just the opening crack of heartbreak with my mom and a few cautious uncertainties with my sister. When I found out they were comparing notes, I was mortified! I felt betrayed and alone. It's not that I intentionally divided the details of my struggle, but sometimes you say different things to your mom than what you say to your sister. I didn't realize it then, but I needed compassionate, pragmatic support from my mom and companionship support from my sister. I wasn't in a frame of mind to rationally navigate the articulation of my needs, and I hadn't even considered a need for boundaries. After all, this wasn't gossip! I was sharing real, down-to-the-core pain. I couldn't bear the risk that their paired chatter could grow to public comments where I would again be told well-meaning clichés like "Just relax! Go on a romantic vacation." I didn't know what I needed to hear, but certainly not those thoughtless words. Achieving a balance between needing to share and needing to protect my heart was a challenge I hadn't expected.

Then there was the time I heard one of the worst comments anyone could say to adoptive parents: "Are you going to try and have one of your own?" As though an adopted child is never really yours! Some people don't realize the moment you hear about your baby or meet your child's birth mother, the bonding is as real as the kicks pushing against a tight, pregnant belly. Those words were daggers stabbed into my heart, and I didn't think I had the strength to display a pretend smile. My heart broke a little more with each condescending remark.

> Achieving a balance between needing to
> share and needing to protect my heart
> was a challenge I hadn't expected.

MY STRENGTH

When an ultrasound revealed a baby girl, I was overjoyed and overwhelmed. I wanted to be a strong and wise woman for her. I began to put pressure on myself to be a perfect female role model. I wanted to give her hope, confidence, peace, and guidance so she would be exactly who God was—at that very moment—creating her to be.

My doctor recommended I journal, and she suggested what sounded crazy: Use my dominant right hand when writing from my own inner voice, but when I was feeling worried about my little one, write with my left hand. She explained that writing from my weaker, unsteady side would slow my mind and bring clarity to my thoughts and feelings. The idea seemed ridiculous, but I gave it a try. It turned out to be sage advice.

Journaling gave me opportunities to maintain sacred conversations. While it was important to have support from other women, it was even more important to honor the vows that had put God, Dale, and me in an unbreakable union. I could write my thoughts when Dale wasn't around and share them with him later. It was a powerful way to protect our marriage because infertility can divide not only your own heart but also the shared heart of a marriage. And those separated hearts can easily stray. This journaling of mine supported our emotional, spiritual, and even physical intimacy.

This regular practice also revealed lingering insecurities from my own girlhood days and helped me overcome them. As the younger daughter in a large family, I had learned that competing for attention was not my strength; that my quietness was perfectly good in God's eyes; and that, in fact, each of us is the apple of His eye and He protects us: "Keep me as the apple of Your eye; hide me in the shadow of Your wings" (Psalm 17:8). Knowing how much God loves me helped me be less insecure with others. I learned to accept my mom's and my sister's support in the ways they were able to share it.

Journaling also led me to seek truth in the Bible and improve my prayer life. At first I wrote out my thoughts, laying the words out to unclutter my mind. Sometimes my wondering transitioned into prayer. The conversational prayers brought questions to mind about God's holy perspective, and I sought clarity through word searches in my concordance. I began to notice how my out-of-balance prayer life involved too much begging for God to make me pregnant, yet the Bible held many profound reminders that nothing is impossible for our God. I spent time alone in silence with God and my journal, and Dale prayed aloud together with me every night before we went to sleep: *God, please bless our family.*

> Journaling led me to seek truth in the
> Bible and improve my prayer life.

My journal writing changed from begging for what I didn't have to thanking God for what I did have, including renewed hope. God was the One I could talk to and the One who listened. He taught me to forgive hurtful words and to resist bitterness. He taught me to look above the present difficulties to His eternal hope. The God who gave Mary a baby named Jesus is the same God who would give me a baby. As I journaled, God showed me both the power of writing words and the power of reading His Word.

MY SCRIPTURE

Give attention to my words;
Incline your ear to my sayings.
Do not let them depart from your eyes;
Keep them in the midst of your heart;
For they are life to those who find them,
And health to all their flesh.
Keep your heart with all diligence,
For out of it spring the issues of life.
Put away from you a deceitful mouth,
And put perverse lips far from you.
Let your eyes look straight ahead,
And your eyelids look right before you.
Ponder the path of your feet,
And let all your ways be established.
Do not turn to the right or the left;
Remove your foot from evil (Proverbs 4:20-27).

These verses provided comfort as well as a healthy reminder to me to listen to God. I needed to listen to Him more than I listen to even my own thoughts. Equally important, the passage reminded me to talk with God even more than those people I love the most. His words can model how I use my words when I'm interacting with others. God's words offer life, protection, boundaries, peace, perspective, and what I needed most during my season of infertility—*hope*. Perspective and hope go hand in hand for me.

6

Things Hoped For

Shelby Doll

MY STORY

From the time I was a little girl, I wanted to be a mom. I dreamed of having a large family and staying home with my kids. I remember feeling anxious when adults would ask me what I wanted to be when I grew up. I would try to come up with a career, which always involved working with kids, believing that "stay-at-home mom" was not an acceptable answer. I carried that belief through my teenage years as pressure mounted to choose a college and career path.

As a high school graduate, I felt lost. I was accepted into two local colleges, but like many young adults, I had no clue what I wanted to do. I struggled in classes that didn't pique my interest, so to avoid the stress of schoolwork and debt, I chose to hold off on college until I could determine a career path. That fall I began working as a receptionist at a surgical center. I loved my job and felt at peace with my choice to forgo higher education. From there, I went on to work at another surgical center and then a local hospital.

When I was 20 years old, my brother took me to buy a cell phone at a store where his friend Carson was working, and I left having met the man of my dreams. Five years later, Carson and I were married. We both desired a large family, and he was supportive of my dream to be a stay-at-home mom. Soon after we were married, we began trying to have kids, and our journey through infertility began. Each month brought on a roller coaster of emotions. Every negative pregnancy test led to disappointment, and the promise of a new month always led us back to hope. Before we knew it, almost three years had passed. After a lot of prayer, we decided to seek medical advice.

I was terrified to talk with my doctor. I didn't want to admit that something was wrong. I didn't want to be told my dreams would never come to pass. I remember sitting in her office and feeling hot when I told her we had been trying for three years, but I had mustered up the courage to squeak it out. She referred me to an ob-gyn, but I felt like God had another doctor in mind. I prayed that God would show me whom He wanted me to see. A few days later, I was walking down the hallway at the hospital where I worked, and I saw an ob-gyn having a conversation with a colleague. He stopped and said, "Good morning!" as I passed, and I heard the Holy Spirit say, "Him." I had heard wonderful things about him, but I had always been hesitant about seeing a physician within my hospital network for personal matters. However, I found out that he had experience with infertility and was also a Christian, so I quickly called my doctor's office and asked them to change my referral to his office.

> I was terrified to talk with my doctor...I didn't want
> to be told my dreams would never come to pass.

A few weeks later, I found myself anxiously waiting in an exam room. My doctor came in and put my mind at ease. He listened to my concerns and shared his own personal story. I left filled with hope and a plan to find out the cause of our infertility. After my husband's tests came back fine, I was scheduled for a laparoscopy procedure.

The day of my laparoscopy, I worried they wouldn't find anything, and the reason for my infertility would remain a mystery. I didn't want to be in that position. When I woke up after my procedure, I saw my husband sitting in a chair. I smiled and asked him the outcome. I will never forget the look of devastation on his face. He explained that I had endometriosis, that both of my fallopian tubes were fully occluded, and that we'd never be able to have children naturally. I sat there stunned, yet filled with indescribable peace.

At my follow-up appointment, my doctor said that I had stage 3 endometriosis. He explained that when he tried to clean out my fallopian tubes, it was like hitting a brick wall. I left his office with a referral to an infertility clinic and instructions to call them to set up my first consultation.

Carson and I discussed the potential costs of infertility treatments, loans, and adoption. We chose to start with the infertility clinic, and while I never felt it was right for us, I reluctantly made the call. The first time I called, I left a message, but no return call came. Over the next three days, I left two more voicemails, and still no one called back. The more I waited and prayed, the more unsettled I felt. That Saturday morning I poured out my heart to Carson. I shared that I didn't feel right about the infertility clinic, that I felt like God had other plans, and that we needed to wait on Him for our answers.

Within minutes of this conversation, my phone rang. It was the infertility clinic calling to say they had a cancellation for Monday morning. After telling the surprised scheduler that we decided not to have a consultation after all, I instantly had an internal battle, wondering if I had made the right decision. But the phone rang again. This time it was my grandma. She said, "Shell, I was praying for you this morning and was given a word. Your baby is on the way. I don't know when, and I don't know how. But your baby is on the way." She also told me to read Psalm 139.

We continued to cling to God's promise, and five months later we were expecting our first child! The following May we welcomed our sweet daughter, Faith, into our family. Our prayers had been answered; our miracle was now a reality. We were told that because we had one child, getting pregnant would be easier the next time we tried.

Right before Faith turned one, we decided to try for our second child. Two months later, we found out that we were expecting again. We were overjoyed! But the day after I had a positive pregnancy test, I began to bleed. Blood work revealed that my HCG (human chorionic gonadotropin) and progesterone levels were low, so my doctor put me on progesterone pills. I went back weekly for blood work. Two weeks passed, and the numbers dropped so low that they determined I was miscarrying our sweet baby. We were crushed.

Experiencing a miscarriage is one of the most awful things I've ever dealt with. For the next 30 days, I experienced bleeding, which was a daily reminder of our loss. I had weekly blood tests to watch my hormone levels slip back to zero. After healing from our miscarriage, we started trying for another baby, but months soon turned into another year. We began to feel that God was calling us to foster care. We got all the information we could and eventually became a certified host family for Safe Families for Children. This is different from foster care in that we care for children when parents are in a temporary crisis, and they do not have family or friends who can help them. Through the organization, we partner with parents and host their children in our home until the parents are back on their feet. In some cases, this program keeps children from having to go into foster care homes. Over the course of seven months, we've had the opportunity to welcome five precious children into our home.

During one of our hostings, almost two years after my miscarriage, we found out we were expecting another baby. On April 3, 2018—two days after Easter—we were blessed with a beautiful baby boy. God is faithful. His promises to us always stand. We need to trust that He will do what He says He will do and stand victoriously even in the battle.

MY STRUGGLE

I am a private person, so sharing my struggles with others has always been a weakness. I'm not sure if it was pride, shame, or fear, but it took us three years before we told even our parents about our battle with infertility. Because we didn't share that information, we faced many crushing conversations with people asking us when we were going to have kids. I always answered with a joke or "Maybe someday," but it was incredibly painful. I know that no one ever meant to hurt us, and we would never hold that against anyone, but it's such an awful feeling when you've been trying to start a family, without success, for months or years.

Finding out that I was the reason we had been unsuccessful in growing our family was very hard. The enemy loves to use times like this to whisper lies into our ears. I felt like a failure: I had let down not only my husband but also my extended family—even though they didn't know what we were going through. I'm thankful I serve a God who shows us when we are believing lies. With much prayer and digging into the Bible, I was able to overcome those feelings and prepare myself for the next steps in the process.

MY STRENGTH

When you are experiencing infertility, the feelings of isolation are overwhelming. You want to tell everyone—yet no one—what you're going through. Because of my tendency to keep my struggles to myself, God was my only option to turn to in times of trial. I clung to God and found my peace and strength in Him. I dug into my Bible and sought out stories of faith, healing, peace during storms, and what Jesus had accomplished on my behalf at the cross. Everywhere I turned I saw the same scriptures and themes of faith. I heard them in music, I heard them in sermons at church, and the Holy Spirit confirmed them in my heart. Even in my darkest moments, I could sense God's hand in our entire situation. My prayer had been that I would receive a miracle, without medical intervention, and that His glory would be revealed in a powerful way. God answered that prayer.

> I dug into my Bible and sought out stories of faith, healing, peace during storms, and what Jesus had accomplished on my behalf at the cross.

MY SCRIPTURE

Now faith is the substance of things hoped for, the evidence of things not seen (Hebrews 11:1).

We can't have faith without hope. During my infertility battle, when hope was waning and my faith felt small, I knew I needed to build my faith. Romans 10:17 says, "Faith comes by hearing, and hearing by the word of God." I dug into my Bible and found hope in reading Hebrews 11, which is filled with stories of the great men and women of faith. Those stories built my faith and brought my walk with God, the Author and Finisher of our faith, to an entirely new level.

7

For This Child I Prayed

Donna Fagerstrom

MY STORY

It was the early seventies. The brother-and-sister singing duo The Carpenters were played on most radio stations and television specials. Their hit song "We've Only Just Begun" was a wedding favorite. My husband and I let the lyrics surround our new marriage. We truly had just begun. High school sweethearts who were now husband and wife, we were experiencing the best of days.

Like many young couples, we glided into this new union filled with promise. This was our new beginning. We had a plan to serve God in full-time pastoral ministry with all our heart, soul, and strength. And we assumed that one day our marriage would naturally lead to a family with children.

In those early years of marriage, we focused on leadership, discipleship, and music. God placed us in a thriving ministry in Muskegon, Michigan, to high school students that started with about 15 kids and steadily grew to more than 200 highly energized teenagers—all brand-new Christians. In the midst of this phenomenal growth, God called us to a youth and music ministry in Denver, Colorado. We settled into this ministry with students devoted to Jesus.

Five years of marriage came and went all too quickly. We hadn't prevented pregnancy, but at the same time we were rather surprised I had not become pregnant. I had struggled for several years with severe cramping that could last an entire month. Realizing this wasn't normal, I scheduled an appointment with my gynecologist. After that appointment I left with news that shocked me and shattered me to my core. The doctor explained that endometriosis was the dreaded culprit. The only temporary cure was to get pregnant and stay pregnant. The dilemma? Endometriosis prevented pregnancy.

We now faced surgery after surgery to remove annoying and painful cysts attached to my uterine wall and ovaries. All of this unplanned aggravation left us feeling devastated by the possibility we may not be able to conceive children.

Weeks later at work, I was convinced I had a severe case of the flu. For the next two weeks, I trotted off to my job as the executive assistant to our senior pastor and youth pastor with saltine crackers and 7-Up at my side. That combination helped me get through the day without feeling the need to excuse myself to the bathroom every 30 minutes. This bad case of the "flu" was just not going away.

One Saturday, without my husband's knowledge, I drove to the pharmacy and purchased an EPT test. Brand-new on the market, it was the first pregnancy test you could take in the privacy of your home. It cost $25 plus tax. My plan was to take the test the next morning, which was Sunday. What was I thinking? My husband and I both had a lot of responsibilities at church all day Sunday, and it took two hours for the test to reveal the results.

But my plan was in motion. I set my alarm two hours early so I could use the test and the results would be ready when we had to get up. Those two hours of sleep evaded me, and when the time was finally up, I hurried to see the results. I looked and exclaimed, "What? That's not possible!" But the test was not lying. It clearly said, "PREGNANT." I was in complete shock as I yelled (no clever reveal or romantic candlelit dinner) to my husband from our guest bathroom, "We're pregnant!" He was doubly shocked, not knowing anything about my little plan.

On Monday morning I went to my gynecologist's office to be tested again. It was official—I was pregnant! My most recent surgery had cleared a path through the endometriosis and made it possible for me to conceive. I was filled with pure joy at this miracle of a baby growing inside of me, but that joy was soon dashed as spotting appeared.

I was in complete shock as I yelled (no clever reveal or romantic candlelit dinner) to my husband from our guest bathroom, "We're pregnant!"

Unplanned doctor's appointments became the norm. I had placenta previa: the baby and placenta are in each other's preferred place within the uterus, which may also be a complication of endometriosis. Placenta previa increased the chances for a miscarriage, and the doctor had me on high alert during the pregnancy. All we could do was hang on to hope, believing that God was in charge—and He was!

I was induced on a Monday morning at 6:00 a.m. The contractions came hard and fast. I labored with contractions a minute apart the rest of the day into the evening hours. The doctor came in that evening at 10:00 p.m. and said he was sending me home. I could not believe it! How would I know when to come back in? The books said, *When your contractions are five minutes apart, go to the hospital.* The response I received was, "You'll know when."

When we arrived back home, our pregnant dog greeted us, and I told my husband she was in labor. He said, "How do you know?"

I replied, "I just do."

So, for the remainder of that night until noon the following day, I had a Norwegian Elkhound lying on my lap giving birth to seven beautiful, healthy puppies, while I leaned back every few minutes to have another contraction. It was a rather delightful distraction, another gift from God.

By noon our prolific dog and puppies were doing fine, so I went upstairs, somehow took another shower, and told my husband to take me back to the hospital. After several more hours of labor, doctors finally performed a C-section at 10:30 that night. To our wildest joy, the doctor laid our beautiful baby girl in my arms. She was perfect in every way. God was amazing.

MY STRUGGLE

Endometriosis was not talked about much in those days. It seemed like every woman could have a child except for me. I began to beat myself up, as if I had done something wrong or could have prevented this endometriosis. A lot of conversations and prayer led my husband and me to believe it was possibly God's plan to be open to adoption, but we were confused and didn't move forward.

Seven years after our daughter was born, I was convinced this would be the year for us to have another baby. We never wanted our children to be seven years apart, but that was the reality we faced. In spite of my positive attitude, we did not have another baby that year. Instead, I was rushed to the hospital unexpectedly for an emergency hysterectomy. When I woke the next morning, the doctor told me the extent and seriousness of the surgery. I was 35 years old and in the full throes of menopause...with no sibling for our daughter.

Grief took me through a deep valley. We once again thought about adoption. We had prayed through that long road before, and here we were at that crossroads again. What God wanted us to do was still a mystery to us. He never provided peace to pursue bringing another child into our home. For reasons known only to our Creator, His plan for our little family was the three of us: my husband and me with one beautiful, blessed miracle. Our family was very complete.

MY STRENGTH

It was a miracle that I was able to carry our baby full-term. We had an army of prayer warriors and an entire church family praying for this baby for months. Our senior pastor's wife was a woman of great faith and kept us in her prayers. Knowing that so many caring friends were covering us in prayer gave me great strength. We were embraced by God and His people.

Another source of strength came directly from God's Word. As I opened my Bible and turned the pages, God spoke to me loud and clear. I was reminded that He truly knew my pain and He was carrying me through this difficult season. Verses like Proverbs 3:5-6 were written not only on the pages of Scripture, but also on my heart. Through these two verses, God told me to trust *Him* rather than rely on my own understanding. He promised to direct my paths as I acknowledged Him, the One who knows me best. God had everything under control. All I needed to do was trust.

MY SCRIPTURE

> *For this child I prayed, and the LORD has granted me my petition which I asked of Him (1 Samuel 1:27).*

This verse is very personal to me. The quiet faith and gentle prayer of Hannah was another gift from God. To see and experience how God brings His children through infertility is more than a miracle. It's His love personified. Like Hannah's accusers, a lot of people were very hard on me. I was considered by some as being selfish to want only one child—but that's not what I wanted! They didn't know my situation or the complications I was facing. There were many times when I didn't understand everything either, but God did. And He was faithful to me...just as He was faithful to Hannah!

8

The Power That Works in Us

Karen Granger

MY STORY

While I was out of town on business, my afternoon appointment canceled, and I found myself with hours of free time in Orlando, Florida. One would think I'd be delighted to have an unexpected day in America's beloved vacation destination, but for some reason I found myself feeling down and depressed.

Then I was struck with the realization: it was the one-year anniversary of our heartbreaking miscarriage. I hate that word—*miscarriage*. Seems too shallow a word for something that causes such deep pain. My husband and I married in our late thirties and joyfully found ourselves pregnant in our forties. When we lost our baby, I felt as though I had lost my one chance to be a mother. The memory hurt so deeply that I couldn't go there.

To avoid the hurt, I let my thoughts wander to a talk about giving that I was preparing for a women's Bible study. During my research, I read about sacrificial giving. As I wandered through the beautifully landscaped walkways of an Orlando resort, I heard God speak to me. I know that may sound strange—How does one hear from God? Is He into texting? In a still small voice, in a way that only He can, the Lord whispered to me, "What about you? Are you willing to sacrifice?"

What? Are You talking to me? I silently questioned. *Sacrifice what?* Then, plain as day, I felt a nudge from God. "Your dream of having a child," God said.

Shock. Sadness. Despair. *Sacrifice my dream of having a child?* I choked back tears. *Sacrifice my dream of having a child?* I couldn't quite digest the thought. *How on earth could You ask such a thing?*

Running from that audacious thought, I quickly fled to my car. Flustered as to how to spend this unexpected free time, I tried to calm myself and headed to a trendy outdoor haven for strolling, shopping, and entertainment.

> In a still small voice, in a way that only He can, the Lord whispered to me, "What about you? Are you willing to sacrifice?"

I considered a movie, but the marquee didn't offer viable options. I glanced at the restaurants, but dinner alone with my thoughts didn't sound appealing. Where could I go to hide from this question about sacrificing my dream? Everywhere I turned, young fathers twirled with darling daughters who were draped in princess costumes. Tourists—parents and kids—were filled with joy and wonder in this magical place. All these happy people exemplified my own dream...that was unraveling. There I was, at the happiest place on earth, and all I wanted to do was collapse in the middle of the street and cry.

I continued trying to drown out God's probing question about my willingness to sacrifice my baby dreams and headed back to the resort. Hoping to drown my sorrow, I ordered a pizza. As I ate away my pain, my hand reached for the television remote control. But God whispered to me again: "Stop running and spend some time with Me." *Spend time with You?* I didn't feel like doing anything with God, especially praying or reading the Bible. Yet, relenting, I dropped the remote.

For the next several hours, I sat on the bed clinging to the 200 thread count sheets, crying my eyes out as I duked it out with the Lord. *Am I willing to sacrifice? Sacrifice my biggest hope and dream for my life?*

"Are you willing?" He repeated.

Am I willing to sacrifice having a family in order to do whatever You want me to do in my life? I can't believe You'd ask that of me. (Tears.) *You're the God who gives us the desires of our hearts. You created me to want children. I love children. I'm great with kids, aren't I? Who am I if I'm not a mother?* (Sobs.)

My heart ached as I struggled to lay all my hopes and dreams at the feet of Jesus. I pleaded, "Other people have children, and they still do great things for You, God. Why can't I? Why do I have to sacrifice this dream?"

Are you willing? He persisted.

It took hours, but finally around midnight, disappointed and drained, I surrendered: *Yes. I'm willing to sacrifice my dream. Why? Because You asked me to.*

A month went by, and I began to experience some health issues. After several visits to the doctor, I learned I was pregnant! *Me? Pregnant? How could that be?* Repeated tests confirmed I was indeed pregnant.

I soon found myself at a prayer meeting that I was covering for a newspaper article on unique prayer groups. The speaker prayed individually for each person in the room. She seemed to have a special gift of knowledge that I'd never witnessed before. She knew the prayer needs of the people without knowing the people themselves. After everyone in the room had been prayed for, I found myself standing before her. She looked at me and said, "You are pregnant. Your pregnancy won't be easy, but hang in there. You're going to have a boy, and he's going to be fine." Just then another woman entered the room and echoed, "That lady is going to have a baby, and it's a boy." I tucked that information away in my heart and didn't share it with anyone.

As we found ourselves with a high-risk pregnancy, though, my husband and I committed the next several months to prayer. I was diagnosed with a blood condition that could be threatening to my life and the baby's. Furthermore, we had no health insurance, I had just experienced the tragic illness and unexpected death of my close-like-a-sister cousin, and two hurricanes stormed through our state.

The pregnancy was difficult just as the prayer warrior had predicted. I only slept through the night once, and throughout these long months—these long nights—the words of the prayer warrior came to mind: "Your pregnancy is going to be difficult, but hang in there. You're going to have a boy, and he's going to be fine."

God met each one of our needs in a miraculous way, and on December 1, 2005, we humbly and tearfully welcomed a beautiful little boy into the world. We named him Luke after Luke 1:37 (ESV), which proclaims, "Nothing will be impossible with God."

My dear friend and mentor responded, "Maybe God just needed to know that you were willing to surrender your plans for His plans, that you trusted Him and His plan for your life. He needed to know your *heart,* and once you surrendered, He blessed you more than you could have ever asked or imagined."

MY STRUGGLE

After experiencing the emotional and physical pain of miscarriage, I was devastated. Being "advanced" in age, I thought my options to have a family were now nil. All my hopes and dreams had died when we lost the baby. I hated to face people and let them know we were no longer pregnant. It's such a difficult subject to talk about. Many friends cannot relate, but surprisingly, once the word of our loss spread, we learned quickly we were not alone. Although that fact is somewhat comforting, it's still difficult to accept you've joined a club you don't want to be a part of.

MY STRENGTH

After many years of walking with the Lord and seeing God do miraculous things in challenging situations, I knew my faith had been growing, and I truly believed I was in God's hands. I knew God would show up in some way, and we would somehow have a "family." Maybe foster care? Maybe adoption? God would show us. And if "family" wasn't in His plan, then He must have another path for using my gifts and talents in the world.

Having a few close friends to share my heart with was so comforting while I grappled with life's plans that were clearly out of my hands. I'll never forget being almost immobilized by sadness after the miscarriage. One day I was sitting on a relative's porch staring out at the water, and a friend showed up with a turkey sub. We barely spoke. She simply sat gazing at the water too. Just the *presence* of a good friend was soothing.

MY SCRIPTURE

> *Now to Him who is able to do exceedingly abundantly above all that we ask or think, according to the power that works in us, to Him be glory in the church by Christ Jesus to all generations, forever and ever. Amen (Ephesians 3:20-21).*

The phrases of these verses are a steadfast reminder that our God is able to do more than we can even think or imagine. He also knows what's best for us. I'm so grateful that afternoon appointment in Orlando was canceled, and the Lord relentlessly wooed me to spend time with Him. I was incredibly disappointed in what I thought His plan was for my life, and I did everything possible to avoid Him. Even while I was wrestling with Him, though, He patiently revealed His grace and love for me. Finally, when I turned to Him in utter despair and with sincere submission, He accomplished more than I could have asked or imagined through the gift of our son.

9

Deeply Devoted to the Lord

Amanda Hope Haley

MY STORY

Only recently have I begun to understand the blessing it is that Hope is my middle name...

My young adulthood went smoothly. I met the perfect-for-me man when I was a senior in high school. David and I married just after we both had graduated from college. We kicked off our new life in a no-air-conditioning, crazy-expensive, five-hundred-square-foot, fourth-floor walk-up just outside of Boston. As soon as I finished my master's degree at Harvard, we ran back to Tennessee where we could afford to buy a cute house and start a family. All was moving according to our plans—until that family didn't arrive as we had scheduled.

Over the next seven years, David and I endured two complete rounds of testing, surgery, and treatments at two separate fertility centers. Despite having some really great doctors (and a few not-so-great ones), we had 96 cycles of failure. We suffered multiple miscarriages. No one—not even my own mother—knew for certain what was happening with us. All of our family and friends were near us in Tennessee, but infertility was too painful, too embarrassing, for David and me to talk about with anyone but each other.

God used those years and that pain to change me inside and out.

Trying to make my body whole, I learned the virtues of clean eating and clean products. Saving money for fertility treatments, David and I became debt free. But these visible improvements were nothing compared to the peace I have now that my hope is only in God. Slowly and sometimes painfully, my nightly prayers changed from "God, get out of my way" to "God, don't let me get in Your way."

I learned that He wants to use me to love the next generation in nontraditional ways I never would have imagined. I find God calling me to mentor people who live in my transitional neighborhood—a place where David and I would not have wanted to raise children. I hope we may one day enrich our nieces' and our godsons' educations by bringing them along on our travels. Maybe God wants me to keep writing and ministering outside my family when He knows I would want to stay home to raise children. Or maybe one day He will call David and me to adopt. The point is, God has a plan for my life and for my desires that fits perfectly with His will.

> My nightly prayers changed from "God, get out of my way" to "God, don't let me get in Your way."

MY STRUGGLE

I've spent most of my life thinking faith is something I must manufacture myself. I suspect this comes from being part of a Christian culture that tends to love making its own rules, such as "Don't drink" and "Don't dance." No matter how strongly I believe that grace is what saves me from my sins, I want *control*. I want to be God. That was humanity's first sin, and it is at the root of every one of mine. If I make for myself a list of rules to follow or goals to achieve, then I create the illusion—or, rather, delusion—that I am in control of my life and faith is unnecessary. That is especially attractive to a type-A control freak like me, but it resonates with every human because none of us want to answer to anyone—not even to God. We want to be our own bosses at work, at home, and even at church.

When we were dealing with infertility, part of me felt as if I did have control. There was something about all the tests and procedures and statistics that gave me faith in what I was doing with my doctors instead of faith in God's plan for our family. And what was my solution to my worst-case scenario? Adoption. If all else fails, I could still "get" that baby.

I am thankful to have a husband who routinely exhibits more faith in God than I do. I may not be thankful for him in those moments when he is right and I am wrong, but I know that he guides our two-person family well. As it was becoming clear that we would not be able to have biological children, I was ready to start the adoption process. And I was shocked when he said no. "An adopted child is not a consolation prize," he told me. "If we are supposed to adopt, then God will call us to do so." David was right, of course. He knew my heart, mind, and motivation better than I did.

Our now-mutual commitment to follow God's plan for our marriage instead of my plans for a larger family seems to be judged by every woman I meet. Casual conversations with strangers follow this pattern: "Are you married? What do you do? Do you have children?" When I answer that we can't have children and don't believe we are being called to adopt at this time, I get either a side-eye followed by strained silence or a bold lecture about how selfish I am to deprive a needy child of our "good home." That implied or expressed shaming—too often from the church—for how David and I feel led to serve God challenges my faith every time. But so far, God has found ways to remind me that I'm here to do His will, not meet society's expectations.

MY STRENGTH

We don't create faith. I can't control how much of it I have because it is a fruit of the Holy Spirit's presence with us and in us. But I am not helpless when it comes to understanding God's will. Contrary to popular belief, God does not have six billion individual wills for the six billion individuals on this planet. Whether or not I have a baby is not God's will. He has one will: humanity's reconciliation with Him.

It was only when I adopted His one will as my one will that my faith grew.

> God has found ways to remind me that I'm here
> to do His will, not meet society's expectations.

Embracing God's will meant releasing my phantom control of my future. But committing to work for His will instead of my own didn't make me just another worker bee in God's Christian hive. God has an individual plan for my life that is specifically designed to further His will. That plan may not involve me parenting my own children, but it certainly brings me the greatest joy imaginable as faith draws me nearer to God Himself.

MY SCRIPTURE

An elderly woman named Anna stepped forward. Anna was a prophetess, the daughter of Phanuel, of the tribe of Asher. She had been married for seven years before her husband died and a widow to her current age of 84 years. She was deeply devoted to the Lord, constantly in the temple, fasting and praying. When she approached Mary, Joseph, and Jesus, she began speaking out thanks to God, and she continued spreading the word about Jesus to all those who shared her hope for the rescue of Jerusalem (Luke 2:36-38, The Voice).

The most inspiring woman in the Bible—in my opinion—is granted only three verses of Scripture. Anna was the widow of a temple priest, and she did not have children. She went to the temple courtyard every day, and she prayed. Because of her faithfulness, God promised her she'd see the Christ Child before she died. At 84 years old, Anna was doing her habitual morning prayer when Mary and Joseph walked in with eight-day-old Jesus. She saw—and maybe held—the Baby, she blessed Him, and then, at some point, she died. That's all we know!

But Anna's story isn't about Anna. Luke didn't put it there so infertile women could identify with her. Her story is in the Gospel because she identified Jesus as the Messiah. The fact that she was childless is secondary. I wish I knew more about her. I wish I knew how she survived month after month of disappointment. I wonder if she was ever pregnant. Did she have a miscarriage? Did she have a baby and then lose him or her to illness?

Anna teaches us something very important. Her three verses of Scripture prove that children are not a reward for a woman's faithfulness to God. That may not be the primary point of the scripture, but I know the Holy Spirit slipped that detail in there to give me hope when I needed it most.

10

In Everything Give Thanks

Mary Hassinger

MY STORY

I grew up in a loud and crazy traditional Catholic family, and I wanted that in my future. I wanted to be surrounded by people whom I loved and who loved me, to know there was always going to be someone there for me, to have the security of similar beliefs and looks and loves. I had all these goals throughout my entire life. I knew that when I got married, I would have a carbon copy of my family—and my husband would want that too.

But Rick and I wondered even before we were married if we might have some difficulties conceiving due to the fact that he and his first wife had been unsuccessful at getting pregnant. While they had not pursued any medical assistance, I was determined to not leave anything to chance. You see, I wanted six, seven, or even eight children—and we needed to get started since, at the ripe old age of 30, I was not a spring chicken! So we scheduled a visit with our general practitioner first, which led us to an infertility specialist...again, and again, and again.

After almost four years' worth of countless appointments and procedures for both of us as well as shots and pills and progesterone suppositories for me, I was getting tired and sad. I was diagnosed with polycystic ovary syndrome (PCOS), and Rick was losing faith in the doctors and nurses, in himself, in me, and in God. He was slipping away from me, from us. I heard him telling a family friend that he was fed up with the whole thing *and* with me. He actually said, "She keeps saying, 'God knows what He's doing' even when she's crying as I jab her with another needle. I'm sick of it." He was no longer joining me for church, and I was obsessively on my knees.

I shouldn't have been eavesdropping, but I am glad that I did. Apparently, we needed to hit a pause/reset button. And that was especially true for me. My desperation to have a large family like the big, sloppy, fun one I grew up in was pushing me to do and think things that I had no business letting into my head—and I hadn't given enough thought to my husband's feelings. And after the thirteenth time of hearing "The test is positive" and the thirteenth time of hearing "I'm sorry" after eight to twelve weeks, I finally had the guts to hit that pause button.

While I knew in my heart that I was meant to be a mother, I also knew that this quest for a biological child was just not going to be the way it happened. So Rick and I began an adoption journey. His best friends had two children with special needs whom they had adopted, and his sister's son had been adopted. Why hadn't we thought this could be God's way for us too? We hurriedly finalized paperwork and had the physicals, the psych evaluations, and the home study completed. Then we hunkered down, fully believing the social worker assigned to our family when she gently said this would be a three- to five-year wait.

I was teaching at my parish school during this time, and the community was one huge family, so everyone seemed to be aware of what was going on in my life. The Prayerful Moms group offered prayers for us every week, and well-meaning advice was coming out of the woodwork via notes and letters and emails and comments here, there, and everywhere. And then something happened. Our school secretary had been chatting with a mom about our hopes to adopt, and this mom knew another mother whose pregnant 15-year-old daughter was determined to release her baby for adoption when the child was born.

Through a complicated series of conversations and calls that I knew nothing about at the time, that young girl's social worker contacted ours, and literally nine months to the day that our paperwork had been finalized and turned in, I was holding our daughter. Our newborn daughter. Thanks be to God! And thanks be to a heroic young girl who decided Rick and I would be perfect partners with Christ in parenting this beautiful child.

I'm not going to lie: I still had huge hopes of adding more children to our little family. However, it was not part of God's bigger plan for us. Rick soon became very ill and passed away. The family I wanted would not grow in the traditional way I had dreamed of my entire life. But grow it did. Hand-in-hand with our daughter, we have been welcomed with open hearts and arms into countless families over these last several years. She has siblings galore, and I have partners in parenting from all walks of life and all over the world. God knew this was the way it was going to be. I should never have doubted that He would indeed bless me with that huge family. A family by God's design.

> The family I wanted would not grow
> in the traditional way I had dreamed
> of my entire life. But grow it did.

MY STRUGGLE

Like so many people, I let myself think, "Why do bad things happen to good people?" After all, I am a good person, and so was my husband. Not being able to easily conceive and have biological children was horrible! I saw infertility as a bad thing that shouldn't happen to good people.

It was no secret that I wanted a large family with many children running around, hanging on to my legs, and dragging their favorite stuffed animals and books behind them. So many people around me—my own siblings, my friends, and many families at school and church—expressed sincere sympathy and sadness at my inability to conceive and my obviously advancing age without any children. I began to feel inadequate and like a lesser wife and lesser woman than the "normal" wonderful ladies I always surrounded myself with. I was even bumping around a little listlessly in my classroom, filled each year with children I had always loved as my own, but now had an odd niggling feeling that I was inadequate for them as well.

To top it all off, I began to wonder if perhaps I had done something wrong in my spiritual life. I began to be that person who wondered why God would be punishing me—and Rick. Rather than trust in God and the ultimate journey He had plotted out for us, I resisted and prayed for change. I should have been praying for stronger faith, for patience, for a deeper love for the One who knew what we needed and could handle—and who knew from the beginning of time about a sweet angel who would need us and our family. God also knew that, with the challenges we would face with Rick's illness, one sweet baby was all I could hold.

MY STRENGTH

I never doubted I would have a family one way or another. I knew that God was not going to ignore that years-old prayer of my heart. Because pray is what I did. That constant conversation I had with my Father, often riddled with questions and begging and pleading and tears of frustration, was also filled with thanks and joy and I-love-yous for Him.

MY SCRIPTURE

In everything give thanks;
for this is the will of God in Christ Jesus
for you (1 Thessalonians 5:18).

I prayed for a baby—or eight—for many years, but I always remembered that it would ultimately be God's will, not mine. I admit, I relied on God's great sense of humor when I often added in my prayer that I sure wished His will were the same as mine, but never for a moment did I forget to thank Him, too, even in my most frustrated and saddest times. I thanked God for Rick and for the wonderful family I had growing up and wanted to duplicate in my own. I thanked God for the great love I know He has for me and for the community of supporters and helpers Rick and I always had.

I carry 1 Thessalonians 5:18 in my heart today as well. The simplicity of this Scripture is part of its beauty. Give thanks: God gave me a beautiful baby (thank You). He grew my family exponentially over the years (thank You). He knew that this one baby miracle was exactly right for me (thank You). His will...thank You.

11

Trust in the Lord

MacKenzie Clark Howard

MY STORY

It never occurred to me that I wouldn't be able to get pregnant. I come from a long line of fertile women. As far as I knew, everyone who had wanted a baby had had one. Some had six. Or eight. I got married in my early twenties, and my doctor told me I'd get pregnant as soon as I wanted to be.

But life didn't turn out quite like I thought it would. Marriage was harder than I expected. We went through some rough seasons where we both knew a baby would not help our situation. I was busy with a career I really loved, and internally I couldn't reconcile how I would manage both that and a baby. As all my friends started having children, it was easier to focus on my demanding job and the fact that I was *choosing* to wait.

I was diagnosed with thyroid disease in my late twenties. My doctors assured me we could get it under control, and plenty of women with thyroid disease have babies. When I was 30, we finally started trying, but then it seemed like one thing after another added stress and disruption to our baby-making endeavors. My mom was really sick. My thyroid tanked again. We put our house on the market.

In the following months, my mom had surgery, and we sold our home. We moved to a small rental and planned to build on property we'd purchased with my family. As these days of upheaval rolled by, some months we tried more diligently than others. But every month was the same: not pregnant.

I started incorporating various fertility measures. Ovulation sticks. Temperature taking. Once I ate a pineapple core because, you know, the lady on YouTube said bromelain could help me get pregnant. It did not.

About a month or so after my mom's surgery, my dad began to have some troubling back pain. He had beaten lymphoma twice before, so any medical issue made me worry. His doctors in their small, rural Midwestern town and even his oncologist in the nearest little city did scans and X-rays and sent him on his way. Finally, they did an MRI and discovered a large tumor on his spine.

I was terrified.

In mere weeks, my daddy retired immediately, and my parents moved in with us in our rented townhouse in Nashville, where God graciously led us to some wonderful physicians. My dad underwent major surgery to have the tumor removed from his spine. We found out his lymphoma had come back in a more serious and potentially life-threatening form.

The stress of all of this put my mom's autoimmune disease into overdrive, which was debilitating for her. I spent days and nights in the hospital taking care of my daddy. Shortly after the surgery, my dad quit all of his pain medication at once, so he could begin intense chemotherapy in preparation for a stem cell transplant.

Baby making was off. We were barely surviving.

The four of us and our three dogs were living in about a thousand square feet. Daddy's hospital bed was in the middle of our little living room. Our lack of space was certainly a first-world problem, but we needed a change. We decided to delay the build and buy a house near the city. We were moving again. This time between chemo treatments and stem cell harvesting.

My hero throughout this time was my husband. Because his job allowed him to take sick time for family, he spent many days driving my daddy to the hospital and sitting with him all day in the chemo ward for his treatment. He, my brother, and I took turns helping when my mom was unable to manage. We worked. We went to the hospital. We repeated. Day after day. Week after week. Month after month.

A wise friend told me that cancer patients speak a special language and understand it in a way that we would not, but that, as primary caretakers, we would understand the language to a degree that most would not. Also, we'd likely feel abandoned and isolated by those who did not speak this language, and we would eventually stop trying to connect with them. I'm so grateful for those people who stuck with us, but mostly, I found what he said to be true.

In my experience, the same can be said for infertility. Those of us who've waited month after month, year after year, and remain childless speak our own language. It's like another club, but not one we wanted to join. And sometimes we feel forsaken. Sometimes people say things without thinking that, at best, leave us scratching our heads. I've had women complain about their pregnancies to me, talk about how they *just keep getting pregnant* or how it was *just so easy* for them that they could pick the month and make a baby. They'll never understand what it's like to know deep in your soul that you were born to be a mother but not be able to hold your baby in your arms.

> Those of us who've waited month after month, year after year, and remain childless speak our own language.

On December 10, my daddy was the grateful recipient of a stem cell transplant, which literally poured new life into his veins. Once we learned that Dad's 30-day scan was clear, I had a conversation with my husband, Josh, that went something like this: "Life's too short to wait any more. I'm done with doctors and waiting rooms for now, but this year I want to become a mother."

And he said, "OK."

MY STRUGGLE

During my dad's illness, I was upset with God. I somehow had an understanding that the rain falls on us all, and this was not God's fault; it was simply a ramification of living in a fallen world. I was upset because I didn't yet have children. I was so young, and my parents were so young to be dealing with this kind of sickness. And yet I felt so old to not have children. I was the stereotypical "sandwich generation," but I was missing half of my sandwich. I was so fearful, and I desperately wanted to give my daddy—both of my parents—grandchildren.

My other infertility struggles, during the months of "regular" life, were simply that I felt angry and alone. It sounds petty, but I got tired of taking my temperature every morning and trying to keep a detailed chart to figure out when I was ovulating. I didn't want to get up and pee on an ovulation stick every day. Why wouldn't my body get pregnant like it was supposed to? I was lonely because it felt like the work was all up to me. My period would be just late enough to get my hopes up. And though conception happens together, inevitably, it seemed like I was always alone in a bathroom stall at work when my period showed up.

It was not supposed to be like this.

MY STRENGTH

When I was in my early twenties, God began planting seeds in my heart to love adoption. After college, I moved away for my first job and rented a room from a wonderful family I met through church. My heart was forever touched by their two precious five-year-old children from China. From that time on, I knew that someday I would adopt, but I thought I'd have both biological and adopted children. My husband typically left the adoption conversation at "Maybe someday."

Someday came for us on the heels of my daddy's transplant. Not long after our conversation, my husband and I went to an informational class on domestic adoption. We felt—at least for the moment—that was not our path, but I kept researching. One night in March, I found a picture of the sweetest little Chinese boy on a "waiting children" website. I showed it to Josh. "What a cutie," he said. I inquired, and though I didn't know it at the time, in the next couple weeks God would throw open the gates for us to finally have a family of our own.

That sweet little boy happened to be with a wonderful adoption agency. On the afternoon of Maundy Thursday, they emailed me his file. "You have three to five days to let us know," the note said. I was full to bursting! Josh was excited but more measured in the beginning: "We have to pray—and find out about his medical records."

"Yes! For sure. We'll ask Jesus. But we're saying yes, right?"

And after prayer and after counsel from one of our dearest friends and physician, both Josh and I joyfully said yes. On that Easter Sunday, we celebrated the new life given to us by our risen Lord, the new life granted to my daddy, and the new life in our family—our son.

In the coming months, our adoption process became the joy and strength of our marriage. The work of infertility had felt isolating to me, but adoption was something my husband and I accomplished together. My husband—who had once said, "Maybe someday"—took off with gusto. His son was on the other side of the world, and he was off to the races to get him home as quickly as possible. This was one of my favorite times of our marriage. Nine months and eleven days after we received our son's file, we got on a plane for China.

> The work of infertility had felt isolating
> to me, but adoption was something my
> husband and I accomplished together.

When I rock my little man in my arms and he reaches up and holds my face with his sweet hands and says, "I love you, Mama," I know with every part of my being that this boy was meant to be mine. It occurred to me that though I have always wanted to be pregnant and bear a child, my desperation was to be a mother. I felt like I had always been a mother; I simply had to wait for God to give me our child. We named him Zechariah, which means "God remembers." God remembered our son, and God remembered us.

MY SCRIPTURE

Trust in the LORD with all your heart,
And lean not on your own
understanding (Proverbs 3:5).

I am a chronic overthinker. I've wasted a lot of precious time trying to figure out things I was meant to leave in God's hands. I don't know why I've never had a baby or why others can't have children at all, and at the same time, I'm in absolute awe that God gave me my precious son. When I find myself spiraling down my rabbit hole of worry, convincing myself something awful is going to happen, or thinking I know the future, I find incredible comfort in Proverbs 3:5. I am not meant to trust my understanding. I'm meant to trust God.

12

He Grants the Barren Woman a Home

Sara M. Howard

MY STORY

I had a wonderful childhood and a great start in life. I graduated from college with a degree in nursing, married my handsome high school sweetheart, and started a job in dialysis—all in my early twenties. We bought our first home and traveled a lot. I was a planner, and everything was going according to my plans and dreams.

Then it was time to add children to our quiet little home. I was ready for the dream of being a mom to become my reality. I was ready for noise, cuddles, toys, nurseries, diapers, and, yes, even messes. My husband and I assumed pregnancy would happen naturally. But during the following months, we experienced the emotional ups and downs of "Maybe this is the month"...only to be disappointed one more time. We became more intentional by using the calendar and turning physical intimacy into a plan. When that failed, we were finally referred to an infertility specialist. We went through many tests and office visits only to be told that nothing was wrong, and we would eventually conceive.

> I was ready for noise, cuddles, toys, nurseries, diapers, and, yes, even messes. My husband and I assumed pregnancy would happen naturally.

We watched with aching hearts as friends and family members were having babies. Many of them did not try long to conceive, and some of them did not try at all. It seemed like everyone around us was having babies. Anger boiled inside of me when I heard moms complain about their pregnancies or how their children were such a burden. As several more months passed, I endured hormone injections, sonograms, and exploratory surgery. After three failed IUI attempts, our heartache brought us to our knees in prayer. But the specialist told us he believed we would still be able to conceive.

After the last failed IUI, I couldn't take the emotional roller coaster any more. My husband and I decided we would no longer pursue medical treatments. We mourned the loss of this dream, the loss of a child whom we so desperately wanted. We did not understand God's plan. We felt deep pain in our hearts that only someone who has yearned for a child can relate to. We were not sure how to move forward with life. And, years later, the hope of conception ended when I suffered painful endometriosis and needed a hysterectomy. How could we—how could *I*—let go of this dream and ever find peace?

After many tearful prayers, asking God to give us peace no matter what our circumstances, we started thinking about adoption. When many little "God things" fell into place at just the right time, we believed that adoption was God's plan for giving us a family. We started the adoption process about six months after our last IUI. One year after that, we held our three-month-old baby boy in our arms, immediately fell in love, and brought him home. Our dream of having a child had finally come true!

We knew right away that we would want to adopt another child. When our son was three years old, we were planning on adopting a baby whose mother had chosen us through an open-adoption agency. We enjoyed the relationship we had developed with her and were counting the days to her labor and delivery. And she was pregnant with a baby girl!

Later in the pregnancy, however, we were stunned to find out the baby had serious birth defects and would probably not live. We were given the option to back out of the adoption. My husband and I believed this baby girl was chosen by God to be our baby, and we would go through with the adoption even if it meant planning a funeral.

Our fragile baby girl was born, and we named her Grace. After 21 days in the neonatal intensive care unit (NICU) and a series of miracles that only God could perform, we finally brought her home—and she stole our hearts. As she grew and became more stable, I wanted to share our miracle story. I wanted our family, our friends, and all the doctors and nurses we met in the hospital to know the whole story. But mostly I wanted God to get the praise and glory He deserved for giving life to our baby girl. I am a nurse, not an author, but I knew I had to tell this story. With the help of a few people God brought into my life at just the right time, I wrote a book called *Tuesday's Grace* that was published in 2011. It tells the story of our miracle baby girl.

We decided our family was now complete. Two beautiful, adorable children—a boy and a girl—who could ask for more? But once again our plan was not God's plan. Four years later, three young sisters in need of a home came to live with us. So we now have a noisy, busy, happy, very messy house that holds a loving family with five children, and each child has an amazing story.

We have experienced modern-day miracles and want to share our story with as many people as possible. Life is difficult and full of emotional ups and downs. But we have learned that if we keep our eyes on God and trust His plan, He will do amazing things beyond what we can imagine.

MY STRUGGLE

Every month brought disappointment. Every negative pregnancy test crushed hope. Then it would start all over again. Our excitement would build as the doctor said, "This month it's going to work!" Then we'd plunge down the steep hill of disappointment—again. The emotional exhaustion affected our everyday lives as well as our marriage. My heart ached every time I had to be around babies. When I saw my husband's tears and disappointment after our last IUI failure, I felt like I could not breathe. I could not bear his disappointment.

I struggled to talk to others about my infertility because the conversation would often end with insulting comments: "Just relax and it will happen"; "You can have my kids"; "Try this position." I knew they were trying to be helpful, but those types of comments were difficult and painful to hear.

I had so many questions for God. I knew my Bible, I knew that bad things can happen to people who love God, but I just couldn't help but wonder why. Why could people who hurt their children have babies, but I could not? Why, God?

MY STRENGTH

My greatest strength came from prayer. I found peace in prayer that I could find nowhere else. When my husband and I were grieving in very different ways and we couldn't talk without getting angry, prayer was my safe place. I could tell God how I really felt, and I shared all of my fears with Him. I knew He heard my cry, and He often gave me a sense of peace.

My sister, who is a psychologist, explained the need to go through the grieving process because infertility is a loss. I found that journaling allowed me to express my true feelings, and I felt relief as I wrote words and thoughts that I was too embarrassed to share with others. I added Bible verses to my journal. I chose verses that gave me strength and hope and healing. I also asked my close family and friends to pray for us. I knew they would, and this helped me feel encouraged and supported even when I did not feel like talking about it.

> When my husband and I were grieving in very different ways and we couldn't talk without getting angry, prayer was my safe place.

As with many difficult situations, time does heal. I often describe infertility like a wound. It starts out painful and tender, but the wound eventually becomes a scar that you notice occasionally.

It has been more than 15 years since we began our journey of infertility. Sometimes I wish I could have birthed and breastfed my children because these amazing, life-changing experiences tend to be talked about in mommy groups. But I choose to focus on the positives: no stretch marks, no postpartum hormone crashes, and my chest area sits a little higher than those of my wonderful breast-feeding friends.

MY SCRIPTURE

> *He raises the poor out of the dust,*
> *And lifts the needy out of the ash heap,*
> *That He may seat him with princes—*
> *With the princes of His people.*
> *He grants the barren woman a home,*
> *Like a joyful mother of children.*
> *Praise the LORD! (Psalm 113:7-9).*

I love that God knew the pain of a childless woman and compared her sadness to that of the poor and needy. Yet, even though childless, she was settled in her home with children. I read this during our trial of infertility, and it gave me much comfort. Then this passage came to life for me! God used sad and painful circumstances for us to grow in our faith and grow stronger as a couple. And now I am a happy mother, settled in my home.

Cling to God. Know that He will lead you to His perfect plan for you.

13

Your Mercy Will Hold Me Up

Darci Irwin

MY STORY

I grew up loving my dolls, and I gloried in taking good care of them. As I matured, though, I went back and forth about whether or not kids would be part of my life. By the time I finished college and was married, I wondered if I truly wanted my life to get all tangled up in motherhood. So my husband and I decided to work for a few years before expanding our family. If only I had known that conceiving on one's own timetable is sheer luxury, we might not have waited...

Once my friends started becoming mothers, my perspective shifted. Holding tiny babies in my arms while visiting friends in the hospital awakened an enthusiasm for motherhood and nurturing. Being married to the greatest future dad the world would ever know, I figured it was a sure bet that Jay and I would be parents. Little did we know that our saying yes to parenting also meant saying yes to a nine-year adventure of not-yet-fertility.

We found ourselves in the waiting room of uncertainty, and it felt like we were the only ones in there. Infertility, at least in our world, was not spoken of freely, so after a year passed with no positive pregnancy test, we felt confused and alone. Then one day, a plus sign graced the scene, and everything changed. The precious, tiny, very loved life inside of me changed mine forever. But life came to a screeching halt when we lost that baby weeks later, and my shattered heart felt irreparable.

My devastation seemingly knew no bounds when two more beautiful babies were both formed and lost in my womb—babies whose faces I'd never see, whose cheeks I'd never kiss, whose toes I'd never tickle, whose hearts I wouldn't know. Three babies were gone, three lives that wouldn't live out theirs. The torture, agony, questions, grief, shame, despair, loneliness, and anger we felt—all of this was acute.

Oh, how I wanted to bring life into the world, through my body, with the love of my life. As our friends were creating and birthing babies, shifts in perspective, conversation, and relationships were happening. Jay and I weren't only losing our children. It seemed we were losing our relationships and our dreams; at times we were losing ourselves. We wondered what would happen to our souls if the answer to our desires remained no.

Unable to accept no as a final answer, I became addicted to hope and set out on a journey to become the healthiest me possible. In fact, I wore a bracelet with "Hope" inscribed on it. For me, hope meant recognizing our suffering but continuing to move forward. I wanted to cultivate a spirit of resilience and not turn inward even though this process wasn't fun, fast, or easy. My heart experienced the worst kind of loss, and I had been given the diagnoses of endometriosis and lupus anticoagulant, yet I believed tirelessly that my body could create and sustain life. No one had told me otherwise! Until I was told we couldn't conceive, I was going to believe we could and we would. And believing was incredibly hard work.

The next several years were spent in hundreds of appointments with a variety of experts, from naturopaths, to acupuncturists, to a therapist, to chiropractors, to a health coach, to medical doctors, and to the couches of supportive friends. I weaned off a medication connected to a diagnosis of narcolepsy I'd received when I was in college. I completed several detoxes. I spent two years in therapy. I radically changed my diet. I had the mercury removed from my dental fillings. I was on hundreds of different supplements throughout the years. You name it, I tried it. For me, hope had to be active. While I felt amazing and knew my body was much more hospitable to a baby, I was exhausted! And so was Jay. Because even after all that work, the dozens of pregnancy tests we had optimistically purchased over the near-decade were visual reminders of the emptiness. The feeling of failure was unbearable, and we experienced that hope deferred truly does make the heart sick (Proverbs 13:12).

For years I vacillated between three worlds: feeling optimistic about bearing a child, being content not having children, and walking the beautiful road of adoption. I had releasing dreams where I was content with any of those futures, but something inside me just knew that biological children were part of our story.

While I was contending with my emotions and trying to make space for my husband's hurt as well, a pivotal conversation occurred. Jay finally looked at me with surrender and said, "Darc, it's not gonna happen." He had never expressed resolve like that before, and I felt something die in me that night. I questioned everything I had believed about hope, and I wept tears of grief. There was no way I could hope for the both of us, so it felt like an end to the story.

Except it was just the beginning. Looking back, I think what died was the pressure to fix myself by myself. That death made a room for life, and a month or so later we found out we were pregnant. Our pregnancy journey is another story of battling doubts and clinging to hope, but we gave birth to a beautiful baby girl, who is now a big sister to another miraculous baby girl (for whom we waited almost a year). The hard and holy work of waiting those nine years paved the way to our family of four, and we can now honestly say, "You have turned for me my mourning into dancing" (Psalm 30:11). I would have waited forever for my girls.

MY STRUGGLE

We had seasons of ebb and flow. At times we couldn't see each other through the fog, and other times one of us carried the other on our back. Making love turned into making a baby, and we didn't realize how infertility can infect a marriage until it was trying to devour ours. Throughout the years we fought hard to be happy and content with each other even if a third member of the team wouldn't come. It was agonizing work.

> Looking back, I think what died was the
> pressure to fix myself by myself.

A child was not some *thing* we desired, but some *one* with whom we wanted to travel— someone to invite to the team; someone to observe and encourage; someone to cheer for and set loose. I feared the loneliness of not having a family, of feeling that I was defective because my body wasn't doing what it was supposed to. I feared not being taken seriously, missing out on conversations about parenting, feeling separated from our peers. I feared overwhelming jealousy that would suck me in and drag me down deep, to where I could no longer see a twinkle of light. While we certainly had good days that sustained us, the overarching theme is that we were hanging on by a thread.

I struggled to hang on to hope when I realized God doesn't promise to give us everything we desire. I struggled to hang on to grace and love when ignorant people didn't understand—like when women would play April Fools' jokes on their husbands saying they were pregnant when they really weren't.

As I felt myself changing, I struggled to hang on to relationships that I didn't want to lose. When anxiety sought to convince me that I was getting too old to have babies, I fought for peace. I fought hard to bless and not curse my body, recognizing that it was not the enemy. I hung on to compassion for myself when I felt defective. When uncertainty sought to deflate our concept of the future, I hung on to a vision of joy. When I realized *waiting* didn't mean "doing nothing," I struggled to hang on to patience. I struggled to hang on to my husband as we navigated this painful process together, at the same time realizing that I needed to make space for his voice, his grief, and his confusion. And when it felt like we were abandoned, I struggled to hang on to Jesus.

MY STRENGTH

When I look back at my nights of gut-wrenching sobs, I see a mother missing her child. The enemy of my soul tried to lure me into stuffing, numbing, and denying my very real, very raw, very human emotions. But the Lover of my soul gently called me forward and outward into the love of dear family and friends. While I wanted to present the façade that I had it all together, not-yet-fertility ravaged me and opened me wide.

> When I realized *waiting* didn't mean "doing nothing," I struggled to hang on to patience...
> And when it felt like we were abandoned,
> I struggled to hang on to Jesus.

Being vulnerable with safe people was my saving grace. Admitting that I desperately wanted to become a mom and then being told that this desire was gorgeous and worthy—rather than foolish and petty—was the most amazing expression of grace. These trustworthy, kind, compassionate people were strong containers for my grief. Because our waiting was so long, the confidantes changed over the years, but there are always good, wise, loving people who will consider it sheer joy to walk with you and point you to the God who knows best and loves most. You need to know you're not alone.

MY SCRIPTURE

If I say, "My foot slips,"
Your mercy, O LORD, will hold me up.
In the multitude of my anxieties within me,
Your comforts delight my soul (Psalm 94:18-19).

Not-yet-fertility brought me face-to-face with the God who sees. When I felt unseen, forgotten, and overwhelmed, God convinced my heart that none of those feelings were true. Instead, I experienced God's empathy and compassion in remarkable ways since infertility was never intended for our souls. After one deflating IUI, I wept in the car, in awe that God was weeping with me. The journey resurrected my heart from believing that God was shaming me, and I now walk with my feet solidly on the truth that our God is always and forever all about love.

14

Yet I Will Rejoice

Wendi Kitsteiner

MY STORY

I was that little girl who was always around babies. I babysat, worked in the church nursery, and held any baby I could get my hands on. If you asked me what I wanted to be when I grew up, being a mother was at the top of my list.

Outside of growing up without very much money, I faced very few struggles. I was awarded a full scholarship to play basketball at a Division 1 university. I never interviewed for a job I was not offered. I grew up in a Christian home, and while I wouldn't have told you I believed good things happen to good people, I had subconsciously started to believe it.

I did not have any lofty career aspirations. I went to college, got my teaching certificate, and started coaching basketball and volleyball as well as teaching English and journalism. But all of this was just temporary for me. My real job would come when I became a mom.

I met John when I was nine years old. We started dating when I was 16 and got married when I was 21. My husband and I relocated to Rochester, Minnesota. Staying on track with the "good things happen to good people" theme of our lives, he was given a spot at the coveted Mayo Clinic Medical School—the single most competitive medical school in the U.S. We were cold...but happy.

Five years into our marriage, we decided we wanted to have children—and the happy life we knew soon began to crumble. I had always had irregular cycles, but I had been told it was due to my athletic activities. After further research, I was diagnosed with PCOS, an ovulatory disorder. The doctors told me that overcoming this obstacle would be relatively easy. While we would need to use infertility treatments, they had no reason to believe those treatments would not be successful.

I began with three rounds of Clomid, but all three were unsuccessful. Then we tried IUI five times, and all five were unsuccessful. The next step was IVF. Four cycles later our arms were still empty.

We walked away from infertility treatments completely broken—both emotionally and financially. However, while we had given up on biological children, we had not given up on God. I strove, every day, to not be bitter. I started a blog to encourage other women on this journey, I started a support group at our church, and I made myself available online and in person to any woman who needed someone to stand alongside her.

Women would often tell me they were worried they couldn't have children because they no longer had the faith to believe it was possible. That's what I was beginning to believe. I wasn't mad at God; I had simply given up believing that I would have children. I had not lost my faith. But I was resigned to a barren womb.

In the fall of 2007, we received a call from Brianna, the flower girl in our wedding. She was now 17 and pregnant and wanted us to adopt her baby. We said yes! On May 7, 2008, we received the call and heard some of the most beautiful four words a parent could ever hear: "You have a son!" A few hours later we were holding our beautiful little boy in our arms for the first time.

When Isaac John was just six weeks old, we found out we were eight weeks pregnant after no treatments at all. To say we were shocked is an understatement! Elijah Luke joined us on January 31, 2009—just about nine months younger than his big brother.

People often make the comment, "Just adopt and you'll get pregnant." While this seems like it happens a lot, our story is actually the exception, not the rule. It doesn't happen often, and I could not believe it had happened to us.

Another surprise was soon on the way. Less than two years after giving birth to Elijah, I found out I was pregnant again. On July 16, 2011, Abigail Grace joined our family. We were thrilled with our family of five—so grateful for the three little miracles that filled our home. But we still had two frozen embryos that we believed were our babies, and we needed to see what God's plan was for those babies.

I had both of the embryos implanted, knowing that they could both be lost. However, one of the embryos survived, and on September 4, 2013, Hannah Joy joined our precious family. We often joke that she is biologically the oldest of the four siblings, despite being the youngest by birth. It makes people really think! After ten years of marriage with no children, God blessed us with four children in five years.

MY STRUGGLE

Before starting IVF, I was required to go through counseling to determine whether I was psychologically able to withstand what I was going to experience. The counselor informed me that I had a "just world mentality," that I thought life would always be fair. I scoffed at this a bit, but upon deeper reflection I realized that she was right. I believed that good things happened to good people and that bad things shouldn't happen to me because I was a good person.

I remember one night when I asked my husband, "Why me?" he replied, "Why *not* you?" It made me pause. *Why did I think I was above this pain? Why did I expect to be immune from suffering in the world?* We sing so many songs in church about trust, and we tell the Lord we trust Him. But when it comes time to hand Him something that is truly, completely out of our hands but dear to our hearts, do we really trust Him? I didn't. And this experience would require me to learn how to do that.

Now that I am on the other side, I can honestly tell you that I never lost my belief in God during all those years of infertility. But I definitely grieved. I definitely doubted His goodness and His plan for my life. I definitely felt forgotten. I strive now, on the other side, to not let women feel alone or unusual in the feelings that engulf them during infertility. It is a very difficult road, and no one should have to journey it alone.

> I strive now, on the other side, to not let
> women feel alone or unusual in the feelings
> that engulf them during infertility.

MY STRENGTH

My first and favorite toy was an old manual typewriter that my parents inherited from one of the customers my mom cleaned for. I loved that typewriter and loved seeing the letters I typed come out on paper. From there I moved to a black computer with green type in my father's office. I would sit there for hours, weaving stories and words together.

I have always loved to write, and infertility meant using the words I loved to find healing. I joined an online support group (www.hannahs prayer.org), I started a support group at my church, and I began blogging (www.flakymn.blogspot.com) at a time when infertility was something many people hadn't even heard of. I didn't want to be alone, and I didn't want anyone else to be alone either.

A few years after our infertility journey came to an end, my husband and I started an adoption organization (www.becauseofisaac.org) to help raise money for childless couples who want to adopt. We were determined to stand alongside—in any way that we could—people who were grieving. I also started writing for a newsletter published by Bethany Christian Services, and I began speaking at MOPS (Mothers of Preschoolers) groups. I was determined to share my story of grief and longing and hope. My goal is to never let a woman feel that she is alone on this journey.

When I began dealing with infertility, it was not talked about much. Technology as we know it today was still coming into its own, and the people on social media weren't sharing pain like they do today. But a lot has changed in the dozen years that have passed since that time. People *are* talking about infertility. They are sharing and making sure others don't feel alone. I like to believe I was part of those initial online crusaders—striving to make sure no woman had to walk these valleys by herself.

MY SCRIPTURE

Though the fig tree may not blossom,
Nor fruit be on the vines;
Though the labor of the olive may fail,
And the fields yield no food;
Though the flock may be cut off from the fold,
And there be no herd in the stalls—
Yet I will rejoice in the LORD,
I will joy in the God of my salvation
(Habakkuk 3:17-18).

I was determined I would not be bitter. If childlessness was the path God had called me to follow, if this was the cross I was to bear, somehow I would do it with joy, worshipping and praising the Lord. Somehow I would bring glory to Him, though this assignment was not easy. I forced myself to pray for every pregnant belly I saw, but I left baby showers and dedications at church to sob in my car. Like Habakkuk, I continued to praise the Lord even when I did not understand why this was happening.

My four children are quickly growing up. I recently turned to my husband and said, "I'm thankful I went through what I did." Because of my experiences I am a more compassionate person and understanding friend. I understand grief and sadness and the loss of a dream. But the journey hurt badly; it was the worst pain I have ever had to face. I know I will face difficult storms ahead, and I pray this scripture will continue to be my theme.

15

More than Conquerors

Ke-Jia Liu

MY STORY

In my early twenties, I assumed that I would get married one day and have kids when the time was right. Back then, I didn't have a natural affinity for kids, but I knew becoming a parent was one of those life experiences that most people go through.

My husband and I got married in our late twenties and decided we'd wait to have kids until we were 30. This would give us time to enjoy our marriage and focus on our careers. But since my cycles had always been a little irregular, in the back of my mind I wondered if we would have trouble conceiving, and I started feeling anxious about our chances.

When we officially started trying to have a baby, my intuition turned out to be correct. After six months, we had no success getting pregnant. I had trouble knowing when I ovulated or if I ovulated at all. After some internet research, I made an appointment with a fertility specialist. At the time, I didn't even know the term *reproductive endocrinologist* (RE). Little did I know I would be dealing with REs for the next five-plus years.

After some testing, we found out that the main issue preventing us from getting pregnant was my inability to consistently ovulate. Our doctor suggested that I start using Clomid. While Clomid helped me grow a few follicles each month and ovulate, we still were not able to conceive after five cycles. We then decided to give Femera a try, but this did not result in ovulation. I was becoming more and more frustrated and decided that maybe the problem was my doctor. The clinic seemed disorganized, and I felt the doctor was not aggressive enough.

I decided to schedule a consultation with a doctor from a well-known clinic in my area. We really liked our new doctor. She explained everything clearly and had a detailed plan that made sense. Her structured plan gave me new hope. Having tried both Clomid and Femera, we decided to try injectables for a few cycles with timed intercourse. If that didn't work, we would then move on to IUIs. Since I responded well to Clomid, I responded extra well to injectables—so well, in fact, that at times we worried about having multiples. I decided that having multiples was better than having no children, so we moved forward. Three cycles of timed intercourse and four IUIs later produced no pregnancy even though each cycle—follicle size, timing, sperm count, ovulation—went perfectly. I also started acupuncture, eating healthier, and taking herbal supplements. I felt sad and hopeless with each negative pregnancy test. I was also starting to feel angry at God. I felt like He was being unfair and that He was against me.

This time also brought other life changes. We moved from New York to California for my husband's career. Because of the move, we took a much-needed break—just for a few months—from trying to get pregnant. But before long I was eager to find a new doctor and start the whole process again. I was 32 and not getting younger. I was frustrated that our infertility diagnosis had turned from "anovulation" to "unexplained" because even with ovulation I was not getting pregnant. After some research, we decided to try IUI one more time and then IVF. The IUI failed, so we moved on to IVF.

My husband wanted to try two cycles of IVF. If we still did not conceive, we would stop trying. We had limited funds, and two IVF cycles were all we could afford. I agreed with my husband because he gave this tiring, emotional journey an endpoint. Even though I knew I would be depressed if we didn't end up having a baby, I could not handle the repeated disappointments and the emotional peaks and valleys any longer. Both my marriage and faith were suffering at this point. I felt angrier and angrier at God. I constantly questioned, "Why does God allow this to happen to me?" I felt cursed.

We started our first IVF cycle July of 2013. I vividly remember the month because when you go through IVF, it's a big deal! Your whole life revolves around a calendar, so you remember the date. I felt ready physically, mentally, and emotionally. I had a group of close friends praying for us. I joined an online Christian infertility forum called Hannah's Prayer during our IUI cycles. In this online forum I found a community of women who understood what we were going through. I had my cycle buddies and my cheering squad ready.

Like many of my previous treatment cycles, my IVF cycle went perfectly. I had a smooth egg retrieval, great fertilization, beautiful blastsocysts, and an uneventful transfer of one embryo. Nine days post-transfer, we found out that I was not pregnant. How could such a perfect cycle result in no pregnancy? I felt angry at my body, and the tears flowed. But after some time to digest the news, I was brave enough to try again—and then again. On our second embryo transfer, I was thrilled to see—for the first time in my life—that second line on a home pregnancy test! But, sadly, a retest showed that the pregnancy was not viable. I spiraled into another few months of depression.

In March of 2014, we did our final embryo transfer from the first IVF cycle. Even though we transferred three blasts, the result was negative. We took a six-month break before moving forward to our final IVF cycle. In September of that year, we started IVF again. The cycle itself did not go as smoothly as the first cycle, and we almost canceled, but our doctor encouraged us to move forward with a Day 3 transfer of two embryos. This cycle turned out to be a success, and our twins were conceived. After more than five years, five IUIs, two IVF cycles, and three frozen embryo transfers, we completed our infertility journey. I am now the mother of twins—one boy and one girl!

MY STRUGGLE

I struggled a lot with bitterness and jealousy during my infertility. It seemed like everyone around me had an easier time getting pregnant. At times, I became angry even at comments from well-meaning friends. Sometimes I had to step out of social situations to protect my heart.

However, I believe my biggest struggle was with the lack of control. I wanted to be able to control my circumstances and timing. Needing to be in control is my biggest weakness. I have struggled with control all my life, and dealing with infertility made me feel out of control. You plan and plan, and then your plans fail in your face.

I believe the root of my struggle with control lies in my not believing my true identity. I felt that I was inadequate and incomplete unless I could control all the details and direction of my life. If I lost control of that direction, then I felt like I was without hope. This is the lie that I believed. Letting go—releasing control—was the biggest lesson I believe God was trying to teach me. He wanted me to trust Him. During the darkest times, I was filled with fear and insecurity about the future. If I had fully trusted God with my plans, there would have been no room for fear.

> Letting go—releasing control—was the biggest lesson I believe God was trying to teach me. He wanted me to trust Him.

I was vocal to God regarding my struggles. I told Him exactly how I felt, and most of the time it wasn't pretty. I knew God heard me, but sometimes He chooses to answer with silence—or what felt like silence. During our years of infertility, I read *A Grief Observed* by C.S. Lewis. In the book, he discusses God's apparent silence during our suffering and puts into words exactly what I was feeling. I felt like God had abandoned me, and I felt hopeless in His absence. Even though He never promised a life free of suffering, I struggled with doubts about God's character. Suffering will bring us to the edge of faith and doubt, but God does not change. He alone is our eternal hope.

MY STRENGTH

My personality is such that it's hard for me to keep my feelings inside. When I am going through hard times, I find it helpful to talk to others about my struggles. Infertility can be a very lonely journey, and without the support of friends and family, I would have found it a lot harder to take each step. Being open and vulnerable allowed me to meet a lot of wonderful women who were going through similar troubles. We were able to learn from each other and support each other through the hardest times. One in eight couples struggles with infertility, and nobody should have to go through this alone. I was thankful that God put specific people in our lives to pray for us, support us, and help us on this journey.

> Suffering will bring us to the edge
> of faith and doubt, but God does not
> change. He alone is our eternal hope.

God taught me many things during our years of trying to have children. I've learned that true joy does not come from our circumstances; it's not dependent on what we have or don't have. And hope is available to us now, regardless of our pain and struggles. If we realized that we are eternally loved and truly treasured by our Creator, then we wouldn't need to try so hard to control our lives. When we accept that truth, we can be freed from whatever is holding us in chains and allow God to take over our paths.

MY SCRIPTURE

We are more than conquerors through Him who loved us. For I am persuaded that neither death nor life, nor angels nor principalities nor powers, nor things present nor things to come, nor height nor depth, nor any other created thing, shall be able to separate us from the love of God which is in Christ Jesus our Lord (Romans 8:37-39).

Today, I focus on remembering that God always loves me and that nothing in this life can separate me from His love. Even our doubts and anger toward God cannot stop Him from loving us. We are the beloved children of God. This is the identity on which we can build our lives, and nothing can take that away. We have the security of belonging to our almighty God, our heavenly Father, even if all the circumstances around us appear to be falling apart.

16

My Portion Forever

Zena Dell Lowe

MY STORY

My struggle with infertility began almost the moment I got married. It was my second marriage, and I was already 34 years old. Not beyond childbearing age by any means, but certainly no spring chicken. That's why, after only eight months of trying with no results, we decided to see a specialist.

She recommended IVF right away. I was shocked. Wasn't there a more natural course we could take? We just weren't ready to take that radical step yet, so for the next two years, we tried everything from chiropractic to acupuncture, diet and exercise regimens, natural supplements and supposed herbal miracle cures, essential oils, and a dozen or more IUIs. It was exhausting, all consuming, and heartbreaking, especially as each month passed with no results. Finally, my husband and I decided it was time to consider IVF, but I was terrified because of all of the moral and ethical considerations. *Would it be wrong for me to take such action? Would I be "playing God"? How would He bless me if I took matters into my own hands? Furthermore, what if they harvested 20 eggs? I wanted to be a mom, but I didn't want 20 children!* I was literally tormented by these questions, and I was terrified that I might be acting outside of God's will.

Fortunately, I had good counsel from a pastor who reminded me that all the mental gymnastics I was doing were the result of my traumatic childhood. I grew up in a very dysfunctional, emotionally abusive home. My parents had divorced when I was only two, my dad was a raging alcoholic, and my mother was a classic codependent. I grew up believing that love was a commodity, an exchange of goods. If you love someone, you give them this or that, and they do the same for you. I had no idea what it meant to be loved unconditionally just for being you. No wonder I had such a skewed perspective of God!

Of course, deep down I knew that God didn't work like that. I knew God would love me no matter what and that my views of Him were flawed because of my childhood. Thus, I sought advice and counsel, and I came to the conclusion that pursuing advanced medical technology was not a sin. So what if they harvested 20 eggs? If God wanted me to have 20 children, then I'd have 20 children. So be it!

And so began the very expensive and time-consuming process of preparing for IVF. There were months of hormone injections, blood draws, and visits to the doctor. In the meantime, my faith was being revitalized. I was relying on God. Leaning into Him. Trusting Him like I had never trusted Him before in my life. It made sense to me why He had allowed me to experience infertility, for it forced me to experience Him in this new and delightful way.

Finally, the day came for the egg retrieval procedure. They harvested 17 eggs. However, after three days it became apparent that only two of the embryos were viable. No need to worry about those 20 children. We were going to have twins! They implanted the perfect, already fertilized eggs inside of me, and I was officially pregnant.

> I grew up believing that love was a commodity, an exchange of goods. I had no idea what it meant to be loved unconditionally just for being you. No wonder I had such a skewed perspective of God!

About a month later, I was getting dressed when I felt a sharp pain. I knew right away that I had lost the babies. I remember lying in the fetal position on the bed, feeling utterly and hopelessly despondent. It was one of the most devastating moments of my life. It hadn't worked. God had failed me. Even after I had totally and absolutely believed.

"Unexplained infertility," they said. "The womb should be a life-giving place, warm and cozy like the Hyatt Hotel. Unfortunately, yours is more like the Bates Motel." Yes, a specialist actually said this to me. Nevertheless, they told us to try the procedure again right away for the best results. And so we did, coughing up another $25,000 and trying to muster up the same hope and faith that we had had the first time around. Of course, that proved impossible. My faith had been shattered. I didn't have the hope that I'd had the first time around. Thus, it didn't hurt as badly when the second attempt failed. The damage had already been done.

"Why? Why have You allowed this?" I railed, which is tantamount to demanding, "Explain Yourself to me!" I think it's natural to ask God such questions in the face of such suffering. And who knows? On some rare occasion He may actually give an answer. But no answer He could have given in those moments would have been sufficient: I simply could not comprehend His ways.

I struggled for a good long while, trying to make sense of it all, trying to give it some meaning. I think this is one of our human foibles. We always want things to make sense. If it had been my fault—if I had been a truly horrible human being—then it would have made sense to me. I knew I was a sinner. I'm not minimizing the heinousness of my sin. It's just that somehow I knew enough to realize that this was not some punishment God had inflicted upon me to make me pay for my sins. Jesus had already paid for my sins in full, so it would be unjust for God to make me pay as well. Furthermore, if only "good" people were allowed to have babies, a lot of babies would never be born. So while I didn't have an answer, I knew what the answer was not. Infertility was not because I was fundamentally bad or unworthy. I knew this was true.

Shortly after this realization, a well-meaning girlfriend came over to offer me comfort. She, too, had struggled with infertility and knew the depths of my pain. In her sincerity, she gave me a book that was about embracing life with a broken heart and empty womb. As soon she left, I threw the book in the garbage. That was not going to be my identity for the rest of my life. My identity was not as a mother, but as a child—a child of the Most High God. Even though I didn't understand why

He had not allowed me to get pregnant, I could affirm that He loved me and that He had a plan for my life that included me being useful to Him in some other way. My task—and my privilege—would be to find out what that purpose might be.

> My identity was not as a mother, but as
> a child—a child of the Most High God.

MY STRUGGLE

In addition to my very real struggle to come to terms with God's will and plan for my life, I struggled a great deal with the issue of adoption. As soon as anyone found out about my struggle with infertility, the first thing they asked was "Have you ever thought about adoption?" This comment was said by well-meaning people, but typically they had no idea the true depths of the pain and sorrow that go along with not being able to have a child from one's own body. Many times I resisted the temptation to respond as sarcastically as possible, "Adoption? Tell me about this thing called adoption!" As if I had never heard of the concept before.

Of course I had thought about adoption. Any woman struggling to get pregnant inevitably does. The problem is that not everyone is called to adopt. While I believe wholeheartedly in adoption, I simply didn't feel like it was God's will for me. I couldn't explain it. I just knew He hadn't called me to it.

Unfortunately, many believers seem to think that any woman who longs for motherhood and can't get pregnant should inevitably adopt. If you tell people you're not interested in adopting, they think you're selfish and stingy somehow, and any sympathy they may have offered because of your struggles immediately evaporates, replaced by a subtle scorn. It's as if they are saying, "Well, you had a way out of this pain and suffering, but you chose not to take it. Therefore, it's really all your fault."

I want to affirm women who might be struggling with infertility to consider whether or not they are called to adoption. I hope they will not be pressured into it. It is a beautiful thing to adopt, but it is also okay to decide not to.

MY STRENGTH

Without a doubt, my strength came from the Word of God. If I had not had Scripture to tell me the Truth, I would have inevitably succumbed to the lies of my childhood—lies about my value and worth—and ultimately to despair. The messages I learned growing up were not easy to release. I had to find verses to memorize and recite over and over and over again so I could combat the lies that so desperately wanted to be believed. I also had to rely heavily on prayer because infertility opens a person up to incredible spiritual attack. It's amazing what Satan whispers to you. He tries very hard to get you to doubt God's goodness and love. Without prayer and God's Word, I could not have survived. They literally gave me life.

In addition to helping me combat the lies, God's Word also gave me direction for my future. If being a mom was not God's will for me, then what was? Through prayer and meditation on God's Word, He gave me direction and a purpose, which He continues to give me even until today.

MY SCRIPTURE

Whom have I in heaven but You?
And there is none upon earth that I desire besides You.
My flesh and my heart fail;
But God is the strength of my heart and
my portion forever (Psalm 73:25-26).

I confess that this verse hasn't always seemed true for me, but it became the cry of my heart. I knew that no one could come before God in my life, so I repeated this verse as a prayer. I also wanted to know what it would be like for this verse to be true—to be so in love with God that He was enough for me. I cannot claim that this is true for me every moment of every day, but I have glimpses, and fleeting moments, when it really is true. It is still the cry of my heart. May my good God be all that I want or need. May He be enough for me—because He is.

17

The God Who Sees Me

Kelly Miller

MY STORY

Having been an overachiever and a people pleaser my whole life, I was eager to fit the mold of a Christian woman when I surrendered my life to Christ in high school. I grew tremendously as a believer when I was in college, but I was also exposed to the dangers of legalism. Many times I elevated following the rules over resting in the gospel of God's grace. I thought that being a godly woman should result in being a godly wife and mother. Being my own greatest critic, I was highly disappointed in myself when I exited college with a degree but without the perfect Boaz husband I had so desperately been praying for.

One year turned into five, which turned into ten. Well-meaning people would ask, "When are you going to get married?" "Are you dating anyone right now?" "Don't you want to be a wife and mother?" Of course I wanted those things! Many times during my singleness, doubt crept in, and I would think that I must be doing something wrong and that is why God was withholding a husband. I thought that I must not be following some rule, or I must have some sort of hidden, unconfessed sin. But what God was trying to teach me was that I am not defined by my title or my role in life, but by my sealed redemption from my Lord. Life was not exactly how I would have planned it (college to husband to babies), but God was all about taking unconventional and messy lives and doing something great.

When I was the ripe age of 31, the Lord blessed me with an amazing husband. Thirty-one might not sound old, but in a Southern Bible-belt church, it was considered ancient, and I was already way behind! I had always had consistent periods, and my mother was "Fertile Myrtle," so I thought that getting pregnant would be easy. At the age of 32, after several months of inconsistent periods, my ob-gyn performed some routine blood tests and determined that I would likely never have children. Mine was not a gradual descent into the world of infertility; mine was a complete nosedive. I was diagnosed with premature ovarian insufficiency, which would quickly lead to ovarian failure. In short, I had busted ovaries, I was not ovulating, and the ticking clock was working against me. After seeing our first reproductive endocrinologist and determining that there was no explanation for why I had developed this condition, we were advised to bypass the less expensive treatments and go straight to IVF.

Bitterness began to creep into my heart, and those same doubts I'd had when I was single began to consume my thoughts. I had already done my time in the wilderness while I was waiting for my husband, so why was this happening again? If God had only brought my husband sooner in my life, we might not have had this struggle to have a family. I felt completely alone and started to withdraw from everyone. I avoided baby showers, pregnant women, Facebook postings about babies, Mother's Day at church, and even my younger brother and sister-in-law who were expecting their first child. Throughout fertility treatments, time slowed down, and every month seemed to take an eternity. After numerous prescriptions, costly supplements, painful shots daily, blood tests, weekly doctor's appointments, multiple failed IUIs, and two failed rounds of IVF, God was making it very clear that my poor little ovaries were not up for the challenge.

My husband and I took a break from treatments, mentally regrouped, and asked the Lord for new direction. Should we consider traditional adoption, embryo adoption, or egg adoption through an egg donor? Even though my ovaries were not functioning properly, my uterus always looked up to par. After a series of events, God made His direction clear: He led us toward egg adoption. Each step of the process unfolded with perfect timing. After the first round of treatment, we transferred one perfect embryo to my uterus. After a grueling ten-day wait, we were given the news we had been waiting to hear for three years: I was pregnant! The pregnancy went well, and I gave birth to a beautiful, healthy baby girl who is the joy of our lives.

MY STRUGGLE

As I was walking the road of infertility, I struggled to believe in God's goodness when I couldn't see it or feel it. After Jesus rose from the dead on the third day and appeared before His disciples, Thomas did not believe that Jesus was actually standing before him as the risen King. That's why Jesus said to Thomas, "Because you have seen Me, you have believed. Blessed are those who have not seen and yet have believed" (John 20:29).

Every time we received a poor prognosis and every month that went by without a positive pregnancy test, I found that I doubted even more the very character of God. Was He really good? Thankfully, not only is our God good, but He is "slow to anger, abounding in love" (Psalm 103:8 NIV). I knew that God does not always protect His followers from experiencing tremendous pain in this life. But when God allowed me to walk through my infertility journey, I suddenly forgot God's faithfulness to His people when they suffer. Like Thomas, I needed God to prove Himself to me in order for me to believe in His goodness during this trial.

MY STRENGTH

When I first found out that getting pregnant was going to be difficult, I felt extremely lonely. It seemed that everywhere I looked, someone was announcing a pregnancy. Then the Lord kept introducing me to women who were walking or had walked this lonely road. I began to see that this road was well traveled by many women around me. I was introduced to a group of women who were going through a Bible study for infertility and loss. These women became my light and my hope!

Each woman had a different struggle with trying to build a family, but we all yearned for the same dream. By God's grace, these women were my strength when I felt like I could not keep walking. They would come alongside me and hold my hand when the road got rocky.

Another mighty source of strength for me were the women in Scripture who lived unconventional lives. Many people believe that a Christian life is supposed to look a certain "perfect" way. Life for these women of the Bible was never perfect, but God used their messy lives to impact the world around them and to encourage me in my journey centuries later. Rahab was a pagan prostitute whom God used to help the Israelites conquer the city of Jericho. Ruth was a young widow who trusted God and left the safety of her own people to remain by Naomi's side. Sarah was a childless wife living in a time and culture where women were defined by their children. Mary Magdalene was delivered of seven demons before walking alongside Jesus during His ministry, and she was present at the cross when Jesus was crucified. Mary of Nazareth was an unmarried, pregnant teenager engaged to be married to Joseph, and she became the mother of Jesus. Clearly, Jesus used unconventional women to make His name great. I pray that God uses my tangled life to represent Christ and give light to other women who are walking this muddy road.

MY SCRIPTURE

> *[Hagar] gave this name to the Lord who spoke to her: "You are the God who sees me," for she said, "I have now seen the One who sees me" (Genesis 16:13 NIV).*

The world of infertility can be a place of nameless faces. You can see countless nurses, doctors, and specialists along this journey. You see the same women sitting in the waiting room month after month. Each woman in the waiting room is trying to stay calm and not show the woman next to her that she is really dying inside. We keep our heads down hoping that no one can see the pain in our eyes. We all walk through the same revolving door to see the doctor week after week. For the doctor, I'm sure the faces and names begin to blur because we are all desperate for the same outcome. I felt lost in this sea of nameless faces. But for God, these faces are His beloved, and He knows each woman intimately.

> Jesus used unconventional women to make His name great. I pray that God uses my tangled life to represent Christ and give light to other women who are walking this muddy road.

Hagar had been forced out into a wilderness of despair and hopelessness. She felt alone and betrayed. But in the middle of this wilderness, God spoke to her. He sought her out as His beloved and reminded her of His faithfulness. He is *El Roi*, the God who sees. God sees and knows each woman who is on this journey. He speaks kindly to her and comforts her in her time of trouble. If you are on this journey, I pray that you turn to the One who sees you. *El Roi* knows your struggle; He knows your heart's desire. Above all, He desires to draw you to Himself and make you whole again.

18

With God All Things Are Possible

Katie Norris

MY STORY

At 16 years old, I woke up with an unbearable pain and was rushed to the emergency room to learn that I had a ruptured ovarian cyst. The physical pain did not compare to what the doctor told me next. "Katie, I want to be honest with you. It is going to be very difficult for you to get pregnant." I remember pleading, "Lord, please let her be wrong. I know that with You, all things are possible."

When I was swept off my feet my senior year of college, I knew I had to tell this wonderful man the truth of what our future might not hold. My future husband listened and graciously encouraged me by saying that we would find our path to our family. We married and began our lives together. While doctors encouraged us to start trying to get pregnant when we first got married, we decided that we didn't want to live in fear and we did want to have the opportunity to build our foundation together. However, the doctor's words were a constant hum in my mind. I had no idea what our journey would look like, but I just had to hold on to hope that God had a plan for our family.

We had great years together making memories, starting businesses, and even filming a documentary about an American hero. Five years later, we knew it was time to try. It was exciting to start this journey, but a year went by and no pregnancy. I really didn't want baby making to become a burden in our marriage, so I tried to be patient. I knew that starting a family takes time for most people, and I knew it might be hard for us.

After the year passed, we were more proactive. We tried three rounds of Clomid, but no luck. The constant roller coaster of my tracking my cycle and guessing about ovulation was getting to be a struggle, so we decided to see an infertility specialist and hoped that he could give us answers.

I will never forget walking into the specialist's office. I felt that I had officially joined the Infertility Club. I tried to distract myself by reading a magazine. A vibrant woman walked into the office with her newborn in tow to introduce the baby to the doctor. I learned that it had taken over five years for them to get pregnant, but they did! I remember the spark of hope her story lit inside of me.

We met with the doctor and both had thorough exams. When we went back to see our results, the doctor wanted to do a sonogram to take a closer look. After two years of no answers from doctors, he looked to the screen and saw something no one else had seen. After various tests, we learned that over six fibroids, five polyps, and a cyst were jam-packed in my uterus. He said that I had been living with a version of permanent birth control all these years. There was no way we could have gotten pregnant. Let's just say I never thought I would be so excited to go into surgery!

Six months went by and still no pregnancy. It seemed every time I hopped online or met up with a friend, there was always pregnancy news. Baby showers were getting hard to attend. I fought to stay positive. I learned to be open to trying new things, looking for anything that could help. I began acupuncture treatments, changed my diet, and visited a holistic doctor and a chiropractor. A friend of mine gave me the best advice that helped me during this season of waiting, and that advice was to go serve someone else. Through my work, I was able to focus on serving others instead of focusing on what I didn't have.

Even though that advice helped, I still had hard moments. One afternoon a close friend called to share with me the great news that they were pregnant after one month of trying. I mustered the best congratulations I could, but when I put down the phone, I finally just let it all out. I let out three years of hope, three years of countless pregnancy tests, doctor appointments, and trying-to-conceive (TTC) diets. I was officially defeated. I cried out to God, "I am so tired. I am trying to be strong, but I am losing hope. Will I ever get the chance to become a mother and carry a child?" This day was such a turning point in my life: I surrendered it all.

A friend of mine gave me the best advice that helped me during this season of waiting, and that advice was to go serve someone else.

A month later, I was on vacation with my husband, and I had a dream that I took a pregnancy test. I told my husband about the dream and said I wanted to take a pregnancy test.

"Will it ruin the trip if it's negative?" he asked.

"Possibly, but this dream was so real," I said.

He replied, "Then go for it!"

I took the test, and the word *PREGNANT* came up so fast! We screamed, cried, and got on our knees to thank the Lord. It was an indescribable feeling. God had thrown our mountain into the sea and given us a miracle! We also learned that our baby would be my parents' first granddaughter after 11 grandsons, and that was the cherry on top!

Carrying our daughter was the honor of a lifetime. Rose was born on April 4, 2016, and she will forever be a reminder of God's faithfulness in my life.

Our journey to Rose taught us both so much. It taught us to trust in God's faithfulness and to find desperate dependence on Jesus. Our fears were gone, and we felt like our struggles of infertility were cleared. When Rose was 13 months old, we were thrilled to learn that we had become pregnant naturally. I almost felt like a fraud in my infertility circle of friends. I became the "We were not even trying!" girl who got pregnant without the emotional pain or ovulation strips.

We went into our seven-week appointment to hear the baby's heartbeat. The room became quiet, and I felt like I was watching a scene in a movie when the parents learn the painful news that things do not look good. We were asked to wait for two weeks to learn if the baby had grown or if there was a heartbeat. The agony of waiting for life or death was excruciating. After two weeks, we learned our baby had gone to be with Jesus, and I had a D&C.

As I write, I am unsure of how our family's journey will unfold. But I am sure that God is in control and that He is good.

MY STRUGGLE

My struggles changed as the seasons of trying to conceive unfolded. I never thought miscarriage would be in our story, but now that it is, miscarriage has become my fear. My first pregnancy with Rose was so joyful and pure. The doctor appointments were fun because I could see her in a sonogram, and she was thriving. I had the complete opposite experience the second time around—and for no known cause. The experience was brutal.

The pain of loss and missed memories has been more challenging than I expected. Just when I think I am better, baby announcements or parents complaining about their child or about their pregnancy trigger deep pain. This year I learned that my best childhood friend was having a baby, and ours would have been born the same month. Over lunch I did my best to keep it together because I would never want to steal her joy, but her growing belly was such a visual reminder of how far along I could have been. I let myself shed some tears after lunch, but I knew I needed to focus on what I do have, and that always gives me strength. I am so happy for my friend, but such announcements can trigger pain and jealousy, and I think this must be a struggle for all of us in the Infertility Club.

I long for the opportunity to experience the miracle of bringing life into this world again, but I know that I must face my fear if we are to try to grow our family. I have found so much encouragement from sharing this struggle with my friends who have suffered a miscarriage and from hearing their stories. There is a community filled with men and women who have suffered a pregnancy loss and who have been changed through the experience. As painful as infertility is, it is beautiful to be a part of a community that is so passionate about family.

MY STRENGTH

There are so many unexpected joys when you face trials. Waiting for Rose was one of the most difficult seasons of my life, but when I look back, I see those three years as a gift. The story that God has written for me has become my strength. I learned the powerful lessons of God's faithfulness and how to pray on my knees with my husband. I developed compassion for the infertility community, and the best gift that my story has given me is Rose. Not a day goes by that I don't think of my journey to becoming her mother. My deepest pain turned around to be my greatest joy.

> The story that God has written for
> me has become my strength.

I am thankful for the trials, for the wait, because that has made motherhood the most precious gift. My husband joked that I was the happiest pregnant person he had ever met. I would tell him, "I am just so grateful for the opportunity to be a mom."

MY SCRIPTURE

> *Jesus looked at [His disciples] and said to them, "With men this is impossible, but with God all things are possible" (Matthew 19:26).*

This verse helped me to remember that nothing is impossible with God! These words provided me with faith to keep trusting during the waiting. These words brought encouragement to my 16-year-old self, and, deep down, I knew that my faithful and almighty God would prevail. This scripture continues to encourage our family. It is our anthem.

19

The Lord Goes Before You

Megan O'Connell

MY STORY

I've loved children my entire life. I earned my degree in early childhood and elementary education, and four weeks after I graduated, I married my college sweetheart. It wasn't long before we started talking about having children. Enough children to field his own baseball team seemed like a good number, my naïve pre-parenthood husband said. Although I didn't want *that* many, I figured if I could keep a classroom of children in order, I could manage four or five. Basically, we had it all figured out.

Even then, it was a huge surprise that December morning when I found out I was pregnant without any tracking or intentionality. *Easy-peasy*, I thought. I had a healthy pregnancy, and nine months later went to the hospital to deliver. My labor quickly took a turn for the worse when my son's cord prolapsed. I had a crash C-section, he required resuscitation, and because of lack of oxygen during labor, he was deemed to have moderate brain damage, which could result in severe physical and mental disabilities, or he could grow to be completely fine. Only time would tell.

We navigated the next three years of specialists and therapists for our son, and after an emotional whirlwind, we were thrilled to celebrate his graduation from therapy with a plate of sprinkle-covered cupcakes. He was healed! We had overcome a huge obstacle—and now onward to smooth sailing!

Or not. We had barely caught our breath from the three unexpected and demanding years when we realized a year had passed since we began purposefully trying for a second baby. Well, you know the drill: a year of trying, and you get slapped with the "infertility" label. But wait. We're clearly fertile. We have a child! How did that pregnancy happen so easily? And that's when we learned about secondary infertility. The kind of infertility that happens when there are no known issues the first time around and then—surprise! Eggs stop maturing or swimmers stop swimming, and people start saying insensitive things like "You should just be grateful you at least have *one*."

Because my son's start to life was so traumatic, I don't take one second with him for granted. But that doesn't take away the desire in our hearts for more children. When I see him practicing baseball, I long for a sibling to pitch him that ball. I wish he had a built-in best friend to sleep on his top bunk and giggle with into the dark and way past bedtime.

We started down the pipeline of infertility treatments with the usual—blood work (his and hers), ultrasound, saline-infused sonogram, hysteroscopy, hysterosalpingogram, and semen analysis—along with visits to a naturopath and all the different approaches that come with that. I began taking medication to make my body do what most women's do naturally. Then I switched to a different medication after the first one made me too sick. The disappointment accumulated as the hormones pumped into my body accumulated too, causing pregnancy-like symptoms with no new life to show for it.

We began IUI and soon discovered fertility issues for us both: male factor and PCOS. With our complications, the fertility specialist gave us less than a 1 percent chance of conceiving naturally or with IUI.

And that's where we are. There's one last hormone treatment my husband can try before we are stuck. While we're open to both IVF and adoption, it's financially out of the question right now. So we're in the middle of the raw. Our hopes to have children close in age are quickly fading, while the question of whether there will ever be another moves to the front burner. It's humbling to realize how we feeble humans are not in control. I know that's the way it *should* be, but frankly *should* and *welcomed* are two very different monsters.

MY STRUGGLE

I'm grieving the shattering of my dreams, grieving the hole in my heart and my family, grieving the loss of any semblance of control I thought I had, and so much more. Grief comes unexpectedly and in waves. I never know when it's going to hit, and I don't know what aspect of my grief will take center stage when it does.

It's a physical hurt one moment and an emotional heaviness the next, and sometimes the lies creep in and try to convince me that it's easier to not feel. That's when I go numb. *Lord, protect me from being numb.*

But the hurt and the numb—these are relentless in the face of infertility. I seem hit with a constant barrage of new baby announcements, a time for celebration and joy at the Lord's miracles, but joy is the last emotion I'm feeling—which then leads to guilt. Instead, those announcements remind me that the nausea and extreme fatigue from a few years' worth of medication were in vain.

What was the purpose of the blood draws, shots, ultrasounds, painful procedures, surgery, and miscarriage? What are these women doing right that I'm not? Maybe I need to pray more. Maybe I just need to lean into Him. *Abide*—the word I've meditated on for more than a year—if I could finally put that word into practice, I might be "blessed" with a pregnancy. But what about all those times I've saturated myself in the Word and pressed my face into my tear-stained floor, offering a raw and humble prayer of desperation? Isn't that, though fragile and meager, one tiny sliver of what it means to abide?

This is where my struggle lies: where grief meets numb. It's at the crossroads of guilt and unworthiness. Unworthiness, though, is the lie I've learned to fight. After all, blessings aren't earned. They aren't given to those whose maturity in the Lord surpasses mine. Blessings are a direct result of grace: undeserved favor. *Undeserved.* While I'm feeling plenty of self-pity for my undeserved infertility, friends are basking in their undeserved pregnancy. Why the Lord chose to "bless me" with undeserved infertility instead of undeserved pregnancy, I may never know. But what I do know is that my soul trusts Him. He's shown me over and over that He's with me now, He's already ahead of me, and He alone deserves the right to bestow grace into my life in whatever way He sees fit.

MY STRENGTH

My strength comes from the constant reminders I find sprinkled throughout life that the Lord is with me and has gone before me.

My strength came in that moment a few days after my first insemination when my son drew a sidewalk chalk picture of me with a round tummy. He's four. He doesn't know about our infertility struggles or any treatments we've gone through. Yet that day, after he finished his picture with yellow chalk, he pointed to the extra circle in the middle of his stick figure and excitedly exclaimed, "Look, Mommy! It's you with your baby!"

My strength came a few weeks later when, just as quickly as I learned I was pregnant, I learned I had lost the baby. A watercolor picture by my son. Three stick figures and a scribble: "I drawed me and Mommy and Daddy and a star. Our whole family!" A star. Our whole family.

My strength comes from the constant reminders
I find sprinkled throughout life that the Lord
is with me and has gone before me.

My strength came when my faith faded after pouring my heart out in prayer, only for the pregnancy to end in miscarriage. It came when—loud and clear—the Lord placed on my heart 2 Timothy 2:13: "If we are faithless, He remains faithful." After such a loss, I was without faith, but He was not unfaithful. My strength came when He impressed upon my heart to name this sweet baby I had yet to hold "Faith." In that moment, it was as if He recognized and validated my loss.

My strength comes knowing that Faith Hokulani (Hawaiian for "heavenly star") is being cradled in the arms of Jesus because He is faithful in heaven as well as on earth.

Every tear, every poke, every hard day, and every good one, too, He is with me. He sees me, and His compassion covers me. His promise that He's always with me isn't an empty promise either. He's got a proven track record. So when my memory begins to weaken and my strength starts to fail, all I have to do is pray that He will open my eyes and tune my attention to the ways He is with me, and it doesn't take but a few moments before my strength begins to return.

MY SCRIPTURE

The LORD himself goes before you and will be with you; he will never leave you nor forsake you. Do not be afraid; do not be discouraged (Deuteronomy 31:8 NIV).

These words are where I find peace despite the unknowns. The Lord hasn't promised me a baby, but He will tromp through the hard times with me. He isn't going to abandon me. He's already there at the end of this story, and He's going to equip me with everything I need to get there.

Our world pits turmoil and peace against each other, but in the Lord, they can be synchronized. Like a candle, the Lord's opportunity to show off is in the darkness. To me, one of the most moving ways He shows off is by providing a "peace...which transcends all understanding" in those times of anxiety, depression, chaos, and the unknown (Philippians 4:7 NIV). For me, anxiety rises when I don't know what is coming or, therefore, how I'm going to handle it. But God's not calling me to know how. He's calling me to be still, and He's calling me to lean into Him and follow the path He's already established.

When I am unsure, God is comfort. When I am fearful, He is composed. When I am anxious, He is peace. And at the heart of the matter, He is really all I need.

20

Saved in This Hope

Grace O'Connor

MY STORY

My husband and I married less than a year after we first met. I almost couldn't believe that I had found someone I was so sure about, whom I loved so much, and who loved me back. Part of what I loved about him was that I knew he would be a great dad. While we were dating, I thought to myself, *He will be an amazing father.*

After we had been married a few years, we decided we were ready for kids. A year went by, and my doctor suggested that we see a reproductive endocrinologist. The initial testing did not identify any specific issues, but the statistics we reviewed with our doctor showed the odds were against us, so we decided to proceed with IUIs. For some reason, I never expected any of them to work, and they didn't. After the third failed IUI, we decided to move to IVF. This time, I just had a feeling it would work, and it did. We had the "perfect" IVF cycle, becoming pregnant after a single embryo transfer. While I had expectations that it would work, I'll never forget the feeling of staring at my first positive pregnancy test. At that moment, I couldn't believe it. I was going to be a mom. My husband was going to be a dad. Adding to the good news, our nurse called to let us know that we had three additional embryos that could be frozen for future transfers. I was already picturing our four children. We'd have a full house!

Our son was born, and we soaked up the joys of being new parents.

It felt like all of the waiting and pain was behind us, and after his first birthday, we decided it was time to try for another child. We transferred one of our three remaining embryos, and I was pregnant again. Our joy turned to grief, though, when my hormone levels didn't rise like they should. For a month, I went in for ultrasounds every few days and was told that the baby had a heartbeat, but it was weak; that the baby was growing, but not like he or she should. At nine weeks, there was no heartbeat. I had pleaded with God to let this baby live, and now this little person was gone. I was devastated.

Months went by before we were ready to try again. We transferred the second of our three embryos, and I was pregnant again. But shortly after we found out we were pregnant—and after I had seen the baby's heartbeat on an ultrasound—I was driving home from work with our little boy in the back seat, and I could feel my stomach cramping. While I tried to tell myself it was normal, I knew it wasn't. By the time we got home, I was bleeding. I sobbed that night: I was certain I had lost the baby, and an ultrasound confirmed my fear the next day. This time my sadness turned to anger. One loss I could handle, but I couldn't believe it had happened again.

We had one embryo left. We transferred it, and the pregnancy test was negative. My dream of a full house of children had vanished, and the disappointment was amplified because we wanted another child not just for ourselves, but also for our son. We wanted him to have a sibling, so we decided to do IVF again. After having gone through two miscarriages, I wanted to do genetic testing on the embryos to decrease the chances of becoming pregnant again with an embryo that wasn't viable. I still remember the phone call from my doctor: we had two embryos, and they were both genetically "normal." We transferred one of them, and I was pregnant. I felt like the darkest year of my life had ended, and nine months later we had another little boy. A brother. Holding him in my arms, I finally felt complete.

A year went by, and we decided it was time to transfer the final embryo. For the first time, I wasn't desperate for a positive pregnancy test. If it worked, it worked; if it didn't, it didn't. I was thankful for our two sons, and I was at peace whatever the outcome. The test came back, and we were pregnant again. At my ten-week appointment, my doctor asked if I wanted to do any genetic screening. I hesitated, knowing that the embryo had already been tested and was "normal," but I decided to have the screening anyway. The call came with the results, and the screening test had detected Trisomy 21. Down syndrome. An amniocentesis confirmed the diagnosis. I was shocked, and I was grieving again, this time for a child God was giving us who wasn't what I expected and whom I didn't feel prepared for. I spent my pregnancy learning and preparing the best I could, and by the day of his birth, I couldn't wait to meet him. They held him up in the delivery room, and he was perfect. Our third and final child, another brother, "fearfully and wonderfully made" (Psalm 139:14).

As I write this, our youngest is two months old and napping next to me. I look back at almost ten years of pregnancy tests, injections, appointments, lab results, ultrasounds, and procedures, and I can't believe we're on the other side. Our journey to becoming parents— from our infertility, to our miscarriages, to our youngest son's diagnosis—wasn't what I would have chosen if I had written the story. But God had a plan that was richer and more meaningful than any I could have written. Our house is full. My heart is full. My husband is the father I saw when I looked at him that day before we were married. And I'm thankful for God's goodness.

MY STRUGGLE

We had a close group of married friends who were all starting their families at the same time we were trying to start ours. One after another they announced that they were pregnant. At one point everyone was pregnant except for us and one other couple. I remember thinking that if they got pregnant, I wouldn't be able to handle it.

> Our journey to becoming parents wasn't what
> I would have chosen if I had written the story.
> But God had a plan that was richer and more
> meaningful than any I could have written.

I was sitting at my desk at work when an email came through announcing their pregnancy. I put my head down on my desk and sobbed. I was angry at my friends for being pregnant. And I was angrier at myself for feeling that way. What type of person can't be excited for her friends? But I wasn't. I was planning my friends' baby showers, ordering invitations, making finger foods, and buying things off other people's baby registries. Every pregnant woman I saw felt like a smack in the face. I didn't want to feel that way, but I did.

MY STRENGTH

Early in our fertility treatment, an email popped up from a friend of a friend, a woman whom I had met only once or twice. She also happened to be pregnant. Her email said something along the lines of "I know this is personal, and I don't expect you to respond to this if you don't want to, but I saw you in the waiting room at the fertility doctor. I know you didn't see me, but I wanted you to know that it took us a long time to get pregnant. If you ever want to talk about anything, I'm here." My husband and I are private people, and we hadn't even spoken with any of our friends or family about what we were going through. But I responded to her email, and she became a priceless source of support and our biggest cheerleader.

MY SCRIPTURE

> *Hope that is seen is not hope; for why does one still hope for what he sees? But if we hope for what we do not see, we eagerly wait for it with perseverance (Romans 8:24-25).*

I am not a patient person. If there is something that needs to be done, I don't see any reason to wait to do it. So waiting for our children was the ultimate test of my patience.

After our second miscarriage, a friend told me that she believed we would have another child and that when we did, it would be the right child, at the right time, for our family. I was frustrated with her at the time. I had lost two babies, and I wanted a child now, not later. Another baby was the only thing I felt could calm my grief. But after our second son was born, I knew my friend had been right: he was the right child, at the right time, for our family.

God had a plan for each of our children, and His plan was better than ours. We just had to wait for it.

21

Do Not Lose Heart

Becky Schrotenboer

MY STORY

Like most young girls, I wanted to be a wife and mother someday, but I also wanted a career. I planned on going to college, earning a degree, and working for a while before starting a family. I met my husband, Scott, when I was only 15. We started dating in high school and continued dating through college. Although we broke up a few times, the breakups were short, and I always knew he was the one! The summer after I graduated, we were married, and I got a job working for an interior design company. I then met a woman who became my mentor and whom I worked with for a few years while starting my own design business.

One day my mentor asked me when we were going to start a family. I told her we were planning to have kids someday, but I wasn't ready just yet. She told me that at age 27 fertility starts to decline. She cautioned me against waiting too long because she wanted to have five children and was only able to have two. Well, I was 27, so maybe it was time to start! After nine months of trying to get pregnant with no results, I talked to my doctor. He said that 90 percent of women get pregnant within a year, so give it a few more months—which we did. I thought that maybe I was under too much stress at work and that eventually I would get pregnant, but I didn't.

We finally decided to meet with a fertility specialist. He offered a few possible explanations for our infertility but no clear diagnosis. We started with Clomid, which did nothing. Then we tried an IUI procedure that resulted in pregnancy. We were thrilled! However, our hopes soon plummeted: the pregnancy ended in a miscarriage at about seven weeks. We tried IUI a few more times with no results. We decided to take a break since we were emotionally and physically exhausted. During that break, I got pregnant naturally, but had another miscarriage at seven weeks. We then decided to take things to the next level with IVF. I took drugs, had shots, and went through a very painful procedure. They were able to harvest 13 eggs, but only two of them fertilized. We had them transferred, but no pregnancy resulted. I wanted to try again, so we put down a deposit, but ultimately decided against it. The emotional roller coaster was too much.

After careful thought, we decided we were done trying. I belonged to an infertility support group where I got to know other women who were going through similar experiences. One of the gals told me she wanted to adopt a child from Colombia. A seed was planted in my heart—which is how God works sometimes. My husband and I went to an adoption information meeting to learn all we could about the adoption process. Scott did not want to pursue domestic adoption because, in our state, the law allows birth mothers six months to decide if they want their babies back. We knew that was not for us. Also, we wanted a younger baby, and Colombia was one of the places where we could possibly adopt a baby who was only a few months old. We had friends who had adopted children from Colombia, and they encouraged us to pursue it. We prayed about it and really felt that God was leading us there.

> A seed was planted in my heart—which
> is how God works sometimes.

Fortunately, my husband was able to take time off from work with pay. So when our four-month-old baby girl was assigned to us, Scott and I went to Colombia for eight weeks. We fell in love with everything about Colombia. We made friends with other adoptive parents from the U.S. and still keep in touch with them. It was a wonderful time in a beautiful land, and we went home with our precious baby girl, Ally.

We knew we wanted to return to Colombia for another child, so we applied for a second adoption. We were matched with a nine-month-old boy, but he was very sick with bacterial meningitis. The doctors didn't expect him to live and didn't want to keep us matched with him if he was going to die. He also developed sepsis, had a high fever, and lost hearing in one of his ears. He was put on seizure medication even though he had only had one. (In the U.S., doctors don't even use this particular drug on children, and doctors don't keep adults on it that long because of neurological side effects.)

We went through with the adoption and traveled to Colombia to meet our son, Will, who was now 15 months. Still very sick, he was one miserable little guy. We were not told to wean him off his seizure medication gradually, so when we stopped suddenly, he went through withdrawal and slept only about two hours a night. Even though he was very sick, I felt like God had given us this child and he was ours regardless of his health issues, the same as if I had given birth to him. Ultimately, we were able to bring him home.

We went back to Colombia for one more child 18 months later. While we didn't make gender requests for the first two adoptions, we asked for a girl this time. God had other plans, though, and we were matched with a five-month-old baby boy. Max was so sweet and chill—a complete joy! God knew exactly who we needed to complete our family.

MY STRUGGLE

One of the hardest parts for me was that it seemed like everyone I knew—and didn't know, but saw—was getting pregnant and having babies. I was constantly going to baby showers, trying to be happy for other moms whose dreams of a family were coming true. I remember going to the mall one day and seeing a very pregnant mom smoking a cigarette and drinking a can of Mountain Dew. "Why?" I cried out to

God. "Why do you let some women have babies and not me?" It didn't seem right. I had always been a highly motivated, type-A sort of gal, who always knew what was next. But during this season of infertility, I felt like I was stuck and couldn't move forward. I couldn't see beyond my heartache and longing. My faith was strong, and I knew God was a loving Father, but I just couldn't understand why this was happening to me. It didn't make sense.

MY STRENGTH

I found strength in my support group. It helped to talk with other women who were experiencing the pain and frustration of infertility, so I didn't feel alone. But I am also blessed with a wonderful sister-in-law whose honest conversations were a turning point for me. One day she said to me, "Becky, if you get pregnant and have a baby, is your life going to be perfect?" Her words were penetrating and made me think. "No, my life will not be perfect if I have a baby." She encouraged me to trust God to see where He was going to lead me on this journey rather than obsess over having children. Her words gave me a different and much more positive perspective.

I was also very grateful for my mom and my mother-in-law who went to Colombia after Scott had to go back to the States before we could bring Will home. I could not have made that trip alone. Will was still very fussy and had only slept for one hour the night before we flew home. He didn't want to sit still and was climbing all over the seats. A woman across the aisle kept telling us what to do, and it was driving me crazy! I told my mom to tell that woman to be quiet or I was going to jump out the window! My mom said, "Don't you dare leave me!" We laugh about it now, but at the time it was rough. God knew that having my mom by my side was exactly what I needed.

MY SCRIPTURE

We do not lose heart. Even though our outward man is perishing, yet the inward man is being renewed day by day. For our light affliction, which is but for a moment, is working for us a far more exceeding and eternal weight of glory, while we do not look at the things which are seen, but at the things which are not seen. For the things which are seen are temporary, but the things which are not seen are eternal (2 Corinthians 4:16-18).

What really speaks to me in these verses is not losing heart. When you are going through infertility, you don't know what's on the other side, but things are going to be okay. Even though *you* know what you want, God may have other plans. Through this experience I learned to rely on God instead of myself. I had never before been in a place where I had to do that.

Looking back, I see this experience as the best thing that happened to me because it taught me to trust God completely and to leave everything in His hands. I cannot imagine my life without our three precious children. Each one is a gift from God. Ally, Will, and Max are meant to be my children, something God knew from the beginning. It took me a little while to realize this, but I know for certain that I am meant to be their mom.

22

Something You Would Not Believe

Shay Shull

MY STORY

Andrew and I had been married for several years. We had a puppy, a new house, two good cars, a savings account, and our own business going, so we we were ready for that next chapter in our lives to begin: parenthood. It was time to become parents. Or so we thought.

After five months of not getting pregnant, I went to see my doctor for some answers. I remember leaving that appointment and calling my mom from the car. I was 25 years old, and the doctor had just told me he wasn't sure I would ever be able to get pregnant. He said that my reproductive system was aging far faster than the rest of my body. I cried and cried and cried.

My doctor didn't mess around with mild fertility drugs. He pulled out the big guns right away. Every day from that point on, I began taking two types of fertility drugs, plus Andrew gave me four shots in my stomach. Between the pills and the injectable medicines, they were trying to make my body capable of being pregnant. A few months passed, and we decided it was time to try an IUI. On Memorial Day 2007, I found out I was pregnant.

Being an overly excited, always honest, never-hold-anything-in kind of gal, I immediately told my entire family and all my friends. We went to the doctor, everything looked great, and my pregnancy was in full swing. I had horrible morning sickness almost immediately. I had every symptom a healthy pregnant gal has.

On June 25, I went in for my routine checkup (I was almost nine weeks pregnant), and they couldn't find the baby's heartbeat. I was devastated. The baby was gone. My D&C was scheduled for the next morning, and that was it. I wasn't pregnant anymore.

Between that day and December 8, I had five more IUIs—all failures. I took so many hormones, swallowed so many pills, and had so many needles jabbed into my stomach, I was a mess. Finally, on December 16, when we received confirmation that my sixth IUI had failed, we decided to proceed with IVF. We filled out the paperwork, paid the money, had the affidavits signed, and picked mid-January to start. It was Christmas, and all I wanted to do was enjoy the holiday season minus the pills and needles to the belly.

On January 16, 2008, I was ready to start the IVF procedure. My doctor called and told me to take a routine pregnancy test before I began my meds. This was something I did frequently since they wouldn't write a prescription until they knew for sure I wasn't pregnant. During my lunch break, I grabbed a pregnancy test and decided to take it at work so that my doctor could call in my prescription. I took it, and it was positive!

I remember staring at it for a long, long time. Fortunately, Andrew and I worked together, so I went into his office and told him my pregnancy test was positive. We both thought it was probably wrong. I called my fertility doctor and told them what happened. They asked me to come in for blood work right then...and lo and behold, I was actually pregnant.

After thousands of dollars, six IUIs, a miscarriage, a D&C, and more drugs than I'll ever be able to count, I became pregnant without any of it. God likes to show His glory, and He does so in unexpected ways. He gave me my miracle baby, and on September 15, 2008, I gave birth to Kensington Kate.

Then God thought He would really make His point clear, and on June 5, 2009, when Kensington was only eight months old, I found out I was pregnant again. Smith William arrived on January 18, 2010, and he was another beautiful surprise!

After all of that money, all of that trying, all of the doctor appointments, and all of the prayers, God gave me two freebies. Kensington and Smith came on the Lord's terms, in the Lord's time, and His plan was exactly what I needed. I just didn't know it before.

Now please don't get me wrong! I am a big believer in fertility doctors. I was blessed with wonderful doctors who loved me and cared for me and did everything they could to help me get pregnant. The bottom line is, they could use all the medicine in the world and create the most perfect conditions for conception, but unless God wants to bring a human being into this world, nothing doctors do will create a baby.

Even though I'm ten years past infertility, I still have a huge heart for moms who can't conceive. Whether you're trying to have your first or your fifth, whether you've been trying two months or ten years, I have an aching heart for you. I pray for every woman who emails me about her struggles. From the bottom of my heart, I am so sorry for your pain. I wish I could tell you that one day you'll conceive a child, but I can't. What I can tell you is that God is in control, the Lord loves you so much, and He has not abandoned His good plan for your life. Trust in the Lord, and He will bless you more than you could ever know.

MY STRUGGLE

I struggled with many things while I was trying to conceive. Every doubt, fear, and anxious thought crept into my mind at some point. It was very hard for me to live in the moment. I kept missing out on the now and the present because I was too consumed with the what-ifs of the future. I let a lot of life pass right by me while I fretted over the unknowns of tomorrow. I wish I could go back and capture that time, but it's gone.

> What I can tell you is that God is in control,
> the Lord loves you so much, and He has not
> abandoned His good plan for your life.

Even though my struggles were very difficult, some good things happened to me through infertility. A friend introduced me to one of her friends who was also trying to get pregnant and having issues. We bonded over our struggles, and it was such a blessing to have a friend in my life who knew what I was going through. Without my infertility struggles, I wouldn't be as close to her as I am today. Without my infertility struggles, I would not be able to relate to the many women who reach out to me. Because of my struggles, I know their pain. I want to use my experience with infertility to give hope and encouragement to women who are facing those same struggles right now.

MY STRENGTH

My personal relationship with Jesus is the most important thing in my life. Every morning when I get up, I set aside a few precious minutes to really sit in the quiet and pray, read my Bible, read some other devotional books, and thoughtfully and purposely prepare for my day ahead while chattin' with the Lord. I could not have gotten through that period of my life without the gracious love of the Lord. He was my constant companion, my place of refuge, and my strength. Even when I showed little faith—even when I was too caught up in my own grief to trust His big picture—He never left my side.

Having a daily quiet time, staying connected to other women in my church, praying, and really seeking God through His Word were all ways that I was able to cope and deal with the heartache in my life. God always gave me the peace I needed every single day.

MY SCRIPTURE

I am going to do something in your days that you would not believe, even if you were told (Habakkuk 1:5 NIV).

This is of my favorite verses in the Bible. Oh, how I clung to this verse! I had absolutely no idea what God was doing, but He was doing big and mighty things and preparing my heart for mommyhood in His perfect timing. Little did I know that, after I would give birth to my second child, God would put it on my heart to be a mother to the motherless. On January 4, 2015, we adopted a precious little girl from China. Then again on September 11, 2016, we went back to China and adopted a second little girl. Now I'm a mom to four kids. All four are so very different, and all four are miracles from the Lord.

23

A Future and a Hope

Katie Cruice Smith

MY STORY

When my husband and I were dating, we worked in our church with children from unfortunate situations. Sending them home each week was heartbreaking, and we knew that adoption would be part of our story someday. But we also wanted a biological child—one who looked like both of us. After two years of marriage, we decided to start trying to conceive, but nothing happened.

About that time, I started having trouble eating. My stomach would grumble with hunger, but I couldn't swallow anything. I also began shaking uncontrollably. One hot day, while covering a story at the zoo for our local newspaper, I began to feel woozy. The next thing I remember, the zoo director was wiping my face with a cool washcloth, and I was covered in vomit. I had passed out. I headed to my doctor, who took one look at my enlarged eyes, swollen neck, and shaking hands and declared, "You have hyperthyroidism."

An endocrinologist diagnosed me with Graves' disease. He was surprised I hadn't had a heart attack because my heart rate was so high. My eyes had become so enlarged that I could no longer wear my contacts. And I couldn't keep food down because of the swelling in my neck. In one month, I lost over 30 pounds.

I was immediately sent for radiation treatment, which would destroy most of my thyroid and force me to be on thyroid medication for the rest of my life. For the treatment, all I had to do was take an iodine pill and be monitored for a few hours. Easy enough—except that I was unknowingly exposed to strep, and due to my compromised immune system, I wound up back in the hospital with streptococcal pneumonia. I was very sick and weak for several weeks.

It seemed like we would never be able to have a baby. I was depressed, but I needed to get my health on track. When we were finally able to again pursue adding to our family, we knew it was time to talk to an infertility doctor.

The news we received was devastating. One of the side effects of Graves' disease is polycystic ovarian syndrome (PCOS), a condition that makes it very difficult to get pregnant. Furthermore, if I did manage to get pregnant, the Graves' disease would treat the baby like a foreign object and cause me to miscarry before I would even know I was pregnant.

We decided to start hormone treatments, although insurance did not cover any of it. I was on Clomid for six months. Each month, I would go back to the fertility clinic for a pregnancy test, only to be heartbroken with each negative. And for each negative, my dosage of Clomid was increased. The hormone therapy was awful. One moment I was filled with love and adoration for my husband; the next moment, I was throwing things at him. And there is no greater mood-killer than tracking your ovulation schedule and body temperature!

The next step was IVF, which would cost thousands of dollars from our own pockets. The doctor was not optimistic. "Even if you get pregnant, there is a very slim chance that your body will be able to hold onto the baby," he warned.

I was crushed. I wanted to be pregnant—to feel the baby moving and growing inside of me. I wanted the swollen ankles and nights without sleep. I wanted to sing to my baby and pat my rounding belly. But we didn't know if we could afford the heartache.

We sought counsel from our parents and our pastor. Was this God's way of pushing us to adopt? We were surprised to find that the costs to adopt were comparable to what we would pay for fertility treatments. And, in the end, we had a much higher chance of going home with a baby.

We were already getting close to our five-year wedding anniversary, and we didn't want to wait any longer than we had to. I had heard about a reputable adoption attorney in our area, so we decided to have a consultation. Just three months later, we were matched with our daughter's biological mother, and our daughter was born just four months after that.

And then the comments began. "I know of someone who got pregnant while they were in the middle of their adoption. I just know it's going to happen to you." It didn't.

"Are you going to try to get pregnant now? It's so much easier after you've adopted." It isn't.

"You should adopt through foster care. It's so much easier, and you are guaranteed to get a child." It isn't, and you aren't.

Our kitchen table had plenty of room for another child. I still longed to be pregnant—just like everyone else I knew. But I was so happy to be an adoptive mom. After two years, we decided to pursue a second adoption.

"You already have one," we were told. "Why go through all of this again? Besides, you need to stop adopting babies. There are many older children in need of a home." The unsolicited advice came from everywhere.

When our daughter's birth mother called to tell us she was pregnant again, we knew that we were meant to keep the siblings together and agreed to adopt this child as well. We now had a boy and a girl, so everyone thought we were done. Everyone except for us. We still had room at our table.

After two-and-a-half years, we started looking into becoming foster parents, but then the phone rang. "She's pregnant again," our attorney's assistant told us. "Would you take this baby as well?"

> Everyone thought we were done. Everyone except for us. We still had room at our table.

How could we say no? Of course, this time we had very little support from friends and family. They thought we were being foolish. They didn't know how we could do it. But we just trusted God. And when our third child came into the world, she was immediately loved by all.

Although I still look for signs of pregnancy each month, I am content being mother to these three darlings, and I have enjoyed fostering ten other children as well. We'll see what our future holds because there's *still* room at our table.

MY STRUGGLE

My biggest struggles were envy and bitterness. So many women were getting pregnant—many who never wanted to be pregnant in the first place. In my circle, getting married right out of college, waiting two years, and having babies exactly two years apart was the norm. I was happy for these women, but I also envied the ease at which they were becoming moms. While they were getting together for playdates, I was trudging to work, watching from the sidelines.

As I was invited to one baby shower after another, the bitterness began to set in. All I wanted to be was a mother, yet God seemed to close that door. Was it some sin that I had committed? Was I being punished? Why would God promise to fulfill the desires of my heart but fail to keep His promise? I couldn't see that God was moving and working in my life to bring me closer to Him. I went through a time when I began to question God's goodness. I knew He existed, but I wondered how much He truly loved me. I was wallowing in so much self-pity that I couldn't imagine the beautiful life He had planned for me—a plan that was completely different from mine!

MY STRENGTH

During each of my adoptions, I committed to spending extra time in God's Word and writing in a journal to one day give to my child. Even if I didn't feel like it, I would sit in the rocking chair in the nursery and cry out to God about how I was feeling. Then I would write to my unborn child. Those quiet moments brought me closer to God and helped me feel connected to my baby even though I couldn't be a part of his growth in the womb.

I didn't even know if we were going to have a boy or a girl when I first started writing, so instead I began each entry with "Dear Child of Mine." Every time I found a verse that spoke to me, I would write it down. I wanted my children to see how God orchestrated their lives before they were even knit together. Even when I couldn't see the promise fulfilled, I could trust in the Promise Maker, who never fails us.

MY SCRIPTURE

> *I know the thoughts that I think toward you, says the* LORD, *thoughts of peace and not of evil, to give you a future and a hope (Jeremiah 29:11).*

While we were going through our second adoption, I was really struggling to trust the Lord. We had not planned for this baby, but we had already said yes and fallen in love with him. About halfway through the adoption process, we were running out of money, and we had no way to get any new baby furniture because our daughter was still using it.

I felt like God was being cruel, to dangle a baby in front of us and then snatch him away. I was searching His Word for some promise to cling to, and I came across this verse that I had been taught since I was a child.

No matter that I was going through infertility and a possible disrupted adoption, God's plan for me was one full of hope, and I could trust Him for my future and for the baby's future. Thankfully, the money came in that weekend, and my church threw me a huge surprise baby shower, supplying all the items we were unable to afford.

I look back now, and I can see that God just wanted me to trust Him—with my infertility, with my children, and with my future. While I may not always understand His ways, He is always good, and He is always faithful to have the best plan in place for me. And for you.

24

God Healed

Melissa Sodoma

MY STORY

Growing up, I was not a girl with grandiose dreams of walking down the aisle, living in a house with a white picket fence, and having a ton of babies with the man of my dreams. I spent my days digging for worms and catching salamanders with my brothers. An independent dreamer, I wanted to conquer the world with a sword in my hand. Even so, there were certain things I expected from life. While I knew that Jesus Christ was Lord over my life, deep inside I believed life should bow at my command, and I thought I had it all together.

I married my college sweetheart right after we finished Bible college. Some of the best premarital advice we received was to wait a few years to have children. We were determined to spend the first three years of our marriage building a strong foundation, taking time to get to know each other on a deeper level, developing our blossoming friendship, and having the freedom to travel before we brought children into the mix.

After three years, we decided it was time. This is where expectations enter the story. I thought I would get pregnant the first month of trying. But month one came and went: no baby. Month two came: no baby. When I reached months four and five, I started to sweat when we still had no baby. After a year, I was in absolute panic. Infertility was not part of "the plan." Infertility happened to other people, not to me.

These thoughts swirled through my mind and created a fear that took root in my soul. For the next eight months, my husband and I went through every invasive test and procedure known to modern medicine only to be told there was nothing wrong with us.

At a time when we should have been relieved and hopeful, though, I felt defeated. There was no answer. There was nothing I could fix—and I was good at fixing things! We were referred to an IVF specialist. As I sat on the cold table in a thin paper gown, I listened to our options with a heavy heart. We prayed for clarity, and both of us felt it was not right for us at that time. Lo and behold, the very next month we got pregnant on our own after almost two years of infertility!

We went on to have a healthy baby boy, Ian. I didn't know if we would be able to have more children, but when our son was one, I unexpectedly got pregnant again. I was in shock and filled with joy, thankful that the shadow of infertility was not going to follow me for the rest of my life.

At my first prenatal appointment, I was so happy to be poked and prodded. But during the ultrasound, everything turned to slow motion. There was no heartbeat. My baby had died at eight weeks old. At that moment I felt numb, but I also felt the indescribable peace of God, a feeling I will remember for the rest of my life. I delivered the baby at 12 weeks in an emergency room. It was the worst physical and emotional pain I have ever endured.

It took a long time to recover from this heart-wrenching loss, but a year later, we were pregnant again with our beautiful daughter Cadence. We wanted a big family, so we tried for another child. When Cadence was almost two, I was pregnant again. This time I lost the baby at seven weeks. Pain was my constant companion, but I kept trusting the Lord. After another six months, loss wreaked havoc on my heart once again. We lost another baby, this time at six weeks. After two miscarriages in a row, I told my husband that my heart couldn't take any more pain. I wanted to stop trying. But God decided that wasn't the end of our story. We got pregnant a few months later and, to my surprise, went full-term. I had another gorgeous baby girl, Tatum.

I felt content with our little family of five...until the Lord put adoption on our hearts. We excitedly went through the long, arduous process of our home study, of filling out mountains of paperwork, and of paying all the fees...when I found out I was pregnant once again. I did not fail to see the Lord's sense of humor in this, especially when I went to my first ultrasound, and they informed me that I was having twins!

> I told my husband that my heart couldn't take
> any more pain. I wanted to stop trying. But God
> decided that wasn't the end of our story.

My amazing little bundles were born eight months later. I had boy and girl, fraternal twins, Elias and Isabel. They have been a special blessing from the Lord. I never imagined having twins would be so hard yet so rewarding. It has been unbelievable to watch their interactions with each other and to see the special and unique dynamic they add to our family.

MY STRUGGLE

I faced many challenges as we struggled with infertility. Because most of our friends got married the same year we did, we were one of the last to start having children. We constantly got bombarded with "So when are you guys going to have a baby?" Their innocent questions cut like daggers a heart that had been longing to hold her own baby for nearly two years. No one ever knew our issues with infertility. At first it was because we wanted to surprise everyone when we did get pregnant, but as so much time passed, infertility became too painful to even discuss. So we struggled alone. We experienced only loneliness and isolation as we walked that road. No one ever talked about infertility, so I felt like there was something wrong with me. Like I was the only one who was feeling these things. Like I was broken somehow because I couldn't carry a baby.

My other struggle was the bitterness I felt every time I saw a pregnant woman walk by. This was also a season of countless baby showers that I had to attend. As I would walk through the door, the excitement of everyone in the room was palpable, but it was dread that overpowered me. When others were laughing and enjoying a happy occasion, I would step out early to sit in my car and release my well-hidden tears.

This bitterness and envy soon turned to guilt and shame for not being happy for the glowing mom-to-be.

MY STRENGTH

Some days I was full of faith and hopefulness. Other days I was deep in despair and could not muster an ounce of hope. I do know that every time I was weak, Jesus was my strength. His perfect peace would come and still my aching heart. We could not have made it through such a painful experience without the Father's relentless love.

> Jesus was my strength. His perfect peace would come and still my aching heart.

My husband and I also leaned on the Word of God. I found hope in the stories of barren women of the Bible like Hannah, Sarah, Rebekah, and Elizabeth. I knew if Rebekah could plead with the Lord for 20 years before she had a child, I could do the same. I knew of God's faithfulness not only from these stories, but I reminded myself of things God had done for me in the past. He is always a good Father, and I knew He would be faithful no matter what the outcome of my story. God is the Author of my life. He alone knows it from the beginning to the end, and He is the One who knows what is best for me. I hung on to this belief with all my heart. I knew during this time of my life that the Lord was bringing me to a place where I could surrender control and simply trust Him.

MY SCRIPTURE

Abraham prayed to God; and God healed Abimelech, his wife, and his female servants. Then they bore children (Genesis 20:17).

After I had spent almost two years standing on God's Word in this season, the Lord brought my husband and me to this passage of Scripture in Genesis 20. It's the story of King Abimelech, Abraham, and Sarah. Abraham told Abimelech that Sarah was his sister instead of his wife because he was afraid the king would kill him in order to take Sarah as his wife. God visited Abimelech in a dream and told him what Abraham had done. Abimelech returned Sarah to her husband, but because of this incident, God closed the wombs of every woman in Abimelech's household. The verse that stood out to me was Genesis 20:17.

It wasn't until Abraham prayed for Abimelech and his household that the Lord opened the wombs of the women and they bore children. After reading this verse and talking to my husband about it, we both felt that God was leading us to start praying for others to have children. For the next month we prayed for everyone we knew, that they would bear children, that their houses would be prosperous, and that their homes would be full of love. I do not believe it was a coincidence that the very next month we got pregnant with our son. It wasn't until we took our eyes off our own circumstances, our own pain, and were filled with love and compassion for others that we finally became pregnant ourselves.

Most people would not look at our family of seven and ever think we endured the pain of infertility, but ours is a story of the loving Father's redemption. The blessing of our five children shows God's redemption of the lives that we lost. His plans are not always our plans, but we can trust that He does have a plan—and it is always good.

25

My Grace Is Sufficient

Stephanie Tait

MY STORY

Children have always been a source of joy for me, and I dreamed of a life filled to the brim with them. My first jobs were "mother's helper" gigs and watching children for moms from my church, which led to volunteering in the church nursery and babysitting on the weekends. In college, I initially majored in political science, planning for a career in politics, but my heart was yanked back by my love for children. So I pursued a double major in psychology and early childhood education with an ultimate goal of working with children who have autism and other special needs.

When it came to having children of my own, the joy didn't come so easily. Infertility encompasses so much more than women who cannot conceive. For me, conceiving came a little *too* easily, but I was losing my babies before they ever drew their first breath. My first three pregnancies ended in miscarriage. My fourth pregnancy brought me the joy of holding my first living baby in my arms. We named him Aiden. Then I had three more miscarriages and two heart-wrenching failed adoptions. My next pregnancy came with a serious and painful heart infection for me, followed by three terrifying months of total bedrest with near-constant episodes of active preterm labor. This baby was a hard-won miracle! We named him Jack.

Three years ago, we were surprised with an unplanned pregnancy at one of the most inopportune and terrifying times in our lives. But just as I started to fall head over heels in love with our unexpected miracle, I had another miscarriage. No matter how many times you've experienced it before, and no matter how unplanned that baby is, the loss never gets any easier. It knocks the wind out of you each time you see "the look" wash over that doctor's face.

MY STRUGGLE

My reaction to each loss varied. Sometimes I would rage at God in anger, feeling betrayed and somehow robbed of what I felt I deserved. Sometimes I was convinced that I must have some sort of secret unconfessed sin in my life and God was punishing me. On a few occasions I even pored over the story of Nathan the prophet telling David that because of his sin with Bathsheba, the child they had conceived together would die. I was convinced this account held proof that God was punishing me for something by robbing me of my children. Other times I found myself trying to "name and claim" my way into children, putting on a seemingly brave face and trying to somehow force God's hand, as if He were now required to give me children because I was claiming them in faith.

Ultimately, these varied reactions stem from a struggle many people have had: I tied the goodness of God to my personal life circumstances. I let the idea sneak into my theology that if we hear examples of God's faithfulness in testimonies of provision and blessings, and those things are seemingly absent in our lives, it means either God wasn't faithful, or someone was being punished. I had unknowingly developed this transactional view of God, the view that good Christians who follow Him have tapped into a guaranteed conduit for blessings here on this earth. So when God consistently said no to the deepest longing of my heart, when He allowed my heart to be ripped open over and over again—no matter how desperately I pleaded before the throne—what did that mean? Was God not really as good as I had believed, or was I somehow unworthy of good gifts or too undeserving to receive the blessing of motherhood?

I had unknowingly developed this transactional view of God, the view that good Christians who follow Him have tapped into a guaranteed conduit for blessings here on this earth.

I also struggled to relate to my husband. For years, I harbored deep-seated resentment toward him because I believed he hadn't cared about our babies the way I had or because he wasn't shouldering enough of the grief. It took many years for me to understand that the very things I took as proof that he didn't care enough were actually evidence of his own pain and of how deeply he loved me. When I felt he was moving on too quickly, under the surface he was just as grief-stricken and traumatized as I was. The truth is, he was desperate to make things better because it killed him to see me in so much pain. While my grief was very outwardly displayed, his grief made him retreat inward, and repeated trauma made his brain shut down in response.

I also struggled with relationships with friends and family who were blessed with the gift of motherhood during my seasons of loss. I harbored bitterness and resentment as well as jealousy. I skipped many baby showers and avoided friends with new babies. I judged their parenting decisions privately in that secret corner of my mind, reminding God time and time again that I was so much more deserving and more capable of raising children, that I would do everything right where these women were so obviously failing. When my turn at motherhood finally came, I had many moments of painful repentance and humility as I discovered I wasn't the perfect parent I always believed I would be.

MY STRENGTH

It's hard to use the word *strength* when I look back over my journey through grief. I have so many points I'm not proud of, so many times I desperately wish I could somehow go back and do differently. Yet in truth, I think my greatest strength was my willingness to embrace my own weakness. I wasn't afraid to admit that infertility was totally beyond the limits of what I could carry on my own. I was quick to confront the much-beloved lie that "God never gives us more than we can handle," replacing it instead with the deeper theological truth that God constantly allows us to experience things so outside our own abilities for the very reason of making those limitations clearly apparent to us—giving us no choice but to cling to Him in desperation.

After my seventh miscarriage, I threw myself deep into the Word of God, desperately searching for truths about the purpose of our pain and asking why He allowed so much suffering in the life of even the most obedient of believers. I came to Him an empty vessel, letting go of everything I had always been certain of and dropping every pretense of having it all together or even remotely figured out. Instead of trying to manipulate God with claims of great faith, I laid my very real doubt on the altar in its place, praying words inspired by the man in Mark 9:24, "Jesus, I want to believe. Help my unbelief."

I won't tell you that He revealed all the answers to me and I'm now at perfect peace. I won't say that I understand all of His will or that I can now share the exact reasons for each of my seven miscarriages and just how they fit into some greater design for my life. I also won't proclaim that, as He did for Job, God returned to me many times over that which was stolen away. None of that would be true. In fact, I still long for a third child whom we simply have no idea how to make a reality.

On the surface level, I'm seemingly no better off than when I first began to pray that "Help my unbelief" prayer. What I *can* tell you is the Lord draws near to the brokenhearted, and He truly does bless the poor in spirit and comfort those who mourn. The greatest intimacy I have ever experienced with Jesus has always been during my deepest pain.

MY SCRIPTURE

> *My grace is sufficient for thee: for my strength is made perfect in weakness. Most gladly therefore will I rather glory in my infirmities, that the power of Christ may rest upon me (2 Corinthians 12:9 KJV).*

The more I explore what the Bible says about suffering, the more I am strengthened in the knowledge that I have never suffered alone, that I've never once been abandoned, that these struggles are just momentary in light of eternity, and that we already know how this all ends: Jesus wins, and we win with Him.

The more I have embraced my own weakness, the more Jesus has empowered me with His strength. The more I have surrendered control, the more He has walked me through things I never would have chosen for myself, yet they were His perfect best. The more I have let go of the need to earn His favor or somehow prove that I deserved greater blessings, the more I've seen Him take the very things intended for my harm and use them for my good.

> The greatest intimacy I have ever experienced with Jesus has always been during my deepest pain.

May the God of the universe meet you during your deepest pain and in your greatest weakness, and may you find comfort as Jesus binds your wounds and weeps alongside you, His beloved.

26

In Your Hand

LaShea Udoaka

MY STORY

I was the daughter who did everything right. I went to college, joined my mother's sorority, and graduated magna cum laude with a degree in chemical engineering. I became best friends with another chemical engineering major who was an Air Force ROTC cadet and transfer student from Nigeria. In 1995, this best friend and I renewed our relationships with Jesus Christ and took our friendship to a new level. In 1997, we married, and I was introduced to two new cultures: Nigerian and the military. We spent the first two years of our marriage acclimating me to both.

The next year, we felt that it was time to start a family. After a few months of nothing happening, we went to the base hospital where we were told it was easier to test my husband since it was less invasive. The doctor said if there were any concerns, he would request a follow-up. I was horrified when we received a voicemail a few days later saying that the doctor wanted to see us. In late March of that year, my world changed forever.

Based on my husband's test results, the doctor informed us that we would have difficulty conceiving. I fell into a resentful funk and stayed there for over a year. I was angry at God, yet wondering where the girl who did everything right went wrong. I cried almost every day and totally secluded myself from everyone I knew. I had no one to talk to.

In the African-American community, infertility didn't seem that common. But my husband and I found out firsthand that infertility does not discriminate, and it swallowed me whole.

In 2000, we moved to another military base, where the doctors recommended that we go to Walter Reed Army Medical Center to enroll in its IVF program. On our first visit, the doctors did an ultrasound on my uterus. We received another blow: fibroids. The doctors immediately scheduled me for surgery to remove the fibroids before they began any IVF procedures.

That summer the fibroids were removed with ease, and we did all the preliminary work for IVF. Walter Reed scheduled us to begin our first IVF cycle January 2001. However, instead of being excited about the prospect of starting our family, I had no peace. With all of the needles and hormones, the IVF process terrified me, and the statistics claimed there was only a 25 percent chance of a successful pregnancy. I spent months in turmoil.

I was still struggling with the infertility and searching for answers to deal with my grief when I stumbled upon Bethany Christian Services and its infertility ministry. I pored over their website, signed up for their newsletters, and finally got the spiritual support I needed. Bethany also offered adoption services, and I began to browse through testimonies of families who had adopted. I was intrigued. I posted questions on their chat room and found myself being drawn to the idea of adoption. When I began dreaming about babies, realizing that they were mine but didn't come from me, and recognizing *I was okay with that*, I knew God was changing my heart.

But there were questions about how our Nigerian family would react. In their culture, your family name was your legacy. Would they accept our adopted children as their own? I got the nerve to talk to my husband about my feelings toward adoption, and thankfully our families were receptive. My husband and I decided to focus on adoption, and never considered IVF again.

God was changing my heart.

In January of 2001, I called the Bethany office and asked for information about domestic adoption. The receptionist began to explain that we would need to attend their information session later that month. I responded with a few more questions and then mentioned that my husband and I were African American and were seeking to adopt an African-American child. When she heard that, she paused and replied, "Don't worry about the informational session! I'm sending you your adoption packet today!"

And thus began our adoption process. We learned that African-American children were the hardest to place. The idea that they are all crack babies is a myth. Unfortunately, there are always more children of color who need homes than there are African-American families to adopt them. That summer, our adoption profile was complete, and on August 2, we got "the call." The next day our son was born.

In Nigerian culture, the family elder names the child. My father-in-law emailed us a list of names, and one stood out as the most appropriate. On August 5, we brought Solomon Iniobong home. *Iniobong* means "God's time" in my husband's language. Four years later we adopted our second son, Samuel Christian Itoro.

As an African-American family, our sons' adoptions are not obvious. We are extra blessed to have sons who actually resemble us. We do not automatically share the children's adoption stories with everyone. God creates each family uniquely, and this is simply our story. We did not "save" them from a life of distress. Their birth families are not dysfunctional or welfare recipients. We are not heroes, and our sons are not victims. We love them as if I carried them in my womb because that is the only way we know how to love them. I am thankful for our journey because it led us to the children whom God intended us to parent.

MY STRUGGLE

When we first learned of our infertility, the news brought me to my knees. I doubted God's goodness. I couldn't understand why He was blessing everyone around me with pregnancies—even women who didn't want to get pregnant! With infertility, you have no control. Also,

I was wary of talking to even my closest friends because they didn't know what to tell me, and, honestly, there was nothing they could say to make me feel better. Sadly, friendships were lost because of my jealousy and my inability to rejoice with new mothers.

For one-and-a-half years I walked in a daze, fearful of meeting people and being asked, "So when are you and your husband going to start a family?" As harmless as that question seemed, it made me leave many events in tears. But I learned slowly that even though I hit rock bottom, God was my Rock at the bottom. God had something extraordinary in store for our future family, but He had to get our attention first.

MY STRENGTH

When the doctors informed me of the fibroids, they also told me that if I had gotten pregnant, there was no way I would have carried the baby to term. While my heart was broken once again, I remember hearing a voice whisper, "This is why." I then realized that, although it pained me greatly to be unable to get pregnant, I do not know if I would have had the strength to overcome a miscarriage, and God knew that.

> I learned slowly that even though I hit rock bottom, God was my Rock at the bottom.

I left Walter Reed that day in pain, but knowing that God had protected me from even greater pain. After returning from Walter Reed, I wrote two names in my Bible: Solomon and Grace. For the first time in months, I felt a glimmer of hope and knew that God would bless us with children who would receive those names.

Once I realized that adoption was the way that God would create our family, I received a peace from Him that is unexplainable. His answer to our prayers for children wasn't no; it was "Not your way." I learned that God's will is more important than mine. Just having the faith of a mustard seed was all I needed. I surrendered my will and replaced it with the trust of knowing that God could do abundantly more than I could ever imagine. As we prepared for our adoption, I found myself closer to God than I had ever been in my life. I found strength in focusing on God's power over our situation rather than on the pain.

MY SCRIPTURE

I trust in You, O LORD;
I say, "You are my God."
My times are in Your hand (Psalm 31:14-15).

My infertility journey led me to understand what trusting God really means. You can't trust God fully and still try to control your life. Surrendering comes first. So I let go of how I thought our family should be created and submitted to God's way. Over the years I have slowly been able to open up and share my testimony with others going through infertility. I believe that if God took me through infertility to share His faithfulness with just one other person, then it was worth it all. Our good God had a purpose for my pain. Our infertility experience reminds me over and over again that, for every situation I encounter, God has a plan for me.

27

He Shall Direct Your Path

Joan Van Wyck

MY STORY

My journey with infertility differed from many other women's journeys because I was able to get pregnant easily. My first pregnancy was an exciting time. I was young and had been married five years. All my friends were having babies, and I was thrilled that I was able to share in this wonderful experience. I never considered that anything could go wrong, especially since I had passed the 12-week milestone.

One weekend, though, when I was four-and-a-half months pregnant, I was not feeling any movement from the baby. I was at a ball game with a friend when my water broke. I went to the hospital, and they sent me home. I was feeling very uncomfortable and tried to rest on the sofa. An urge to push made me rush to the bathroom, where I miscarried my baby boy. I can vividly recall every detail of that devastating experience. Within a few months, I became pregnant again. But this pregnancy ended in a miscarriage after only two months.

I soon found myself pregnant for the third time. This pregnancy was going very well, and I was within three weeks of my due date. I was out with a friend when my water broke. I expectantly headed to the hospital, eager to hold our new baby in my arms. But as the nurse began checking for the baby's heartbeat, I knew something was wrong. After 20 minutes of desperately searching for a beating heart, the nurse left the room. The doctor came in and confirmed what I already knew: my baby had died. I delivered a stillborn baby boy and never held him in my arms.

My husband and I decided to try one last time. When I became pregnant for the fourth time, my doctor advised me to seek the help of a high-risk specialist, which I did. I prayed so hard for this child! Seven months into the pregnancy, during a scheduled stress test, my doctor explained that the baby's heartbeat was failing, and an emergency C-section was performed. Brant James was born weighing only two pounds, two ounces, and soon dropped to one pound, ten ounces. From the beginning I knew Brant was going to have major difficulties. He was diagnosed with microcephaly—a congenital condition associated with incomplete brain development. We took him home when he was three months old, weighing just four pounds.

Brant didn't smile or interact with us. He never learned to sit up or crawl. He never walked or talked. It would take me at least two hours to feed him, and he choked often. When he woke up during the night, I would go into the nursery and just hold him. He had some rare moments of laughter that were priceless. Even though he didn't know me like other babies know their moms, I loved him as much as any mother could love her child.

My husband and I decided we would no longer try to conceive. Caring for Brant was all I could do. When he was seven years old, we prayed about adopting a baby, and God answered our prayers very quickly. On a Wednesday afternoon in November, we were in an attorney's office, making plans to adopt a baby who would be born in May. Four days after that appointment, Brant died from pneumonia. Six months after Brant passed away, we held a newborn baby girl in our arms and brought her home to be our precious daughter. Our hearts began to heal.

MY STRUGGLE

My struggle with infertility took place more than 35 years ago. It was a time before the internet allowed women to research questions and answers regarding pregnancies or receive support when a miscarriage ended hopes and dreams. I felt completely alone. I was the only person in my circle of friends who had suffered a miscarriage, and my friends didn't know how to respond to me. *Infertility* was not a word in anyone's daily vocabulary, and miscarriages were kept quiet and not openly discussed. I was sad, hurt, and unable to understand why God was not answering my prayers for a child.

I felt like no one could relate to my painful experiences. No one was there to acknowledge or give credence to my feelings. There were days when the reality of what had occurred would enter my mind, and I just wanted to crawl back into bed and retreat into the escape that sleep could provide. I had no motivation to start my day, and I was overwhelmed with sadness. I realize now that those were symptoms of depression.

The first time I ventured out after delivering my stillborn son, I ran into an acquaintance with whom I had worked. She was excited to see I was no longer pregnant and asked about my new baby. I didn't have the emotional strength to respond to her, so I turned away and walked out of the store. My mom was with me that day, so she explained to the woman what had happened.

> I had very few resources to help me
> cope with my sadness and loss.

I didn't want to go out after that, but I realized staying within the protection of my home was not a long-term solution. I had very few resources to help me cope with my sadness and loss. Back then, professional counseling was not covered by insurance, and we couldn't afford it. Besides, I had been taught that my faith and trust in God would see me through my difficulties and that seeking help from a counselor was a sign of weakness. I was taught from Psalm 46 that God is my "refuge and strength" (verse 1). People often quoted Romans 8:28, reminding me that "all things work together for good to those who love God." I truly believed those verses and knew that God would give me comfort and hope, but as I look back, I know that a Christian counselor could have helped me better navigate the grieving process. I'm thankful that women today have some options I didn't have.

MY STRENGTH

Dealing with our reality was a lengthy and painful process. It was impossible to not be emotionally affected by our circumstances and tragic loss. But even though I was young, I had a strong faith in God that had been passed down to me by my parents. They had lived in the Netherlands during World War II and then moved to South Africa after the war. They had very little money and left family and friends behind. They eventually moved to Wisconsin in 1955, ready to learn a new language, adapt to a new culture, and start a new life. Through challenging experiences, my parents showed me that God loves and takes care of His people. Their example of love and faith in God, and their positive outlook during trying times, gave me the inner strength and faith to face my own challenges.

I had also seen God work in my life in our early years of marriage. My husband and I met in college in Michigan. After we graduated, we decided to move since neither of us had family in Michigan. With no money in our pockets, no job prospects, and no place to live, we stepped out in faith, loaded up everything we owned in our pickup truck—including our blond collie—and drove south until we reached the state of Florida. In time, God provided everything we needed—jobs, home, friends, and church. So as I faced infertility, I knew in my heart that the God who took care of my parents, and who provided for us in Florida, was the same God who was right beside me and would continue to be right beside me each step of the way during this difficult journey. I knew He loved me, and I knew He would take care of me.

MY SCRIPTURE

Trust in the LORD with all your heart,
And lean not on your own understanding;
In all your ways acknowledge Him,
And He shall direct your paths (Proverbs 3:5-6).

I believe that difficult times and uncertainties in our lives are stepping-stones and that God uses each stepping-stone circumstance to bring us closer to a point of trusting Him completely. We build on the difficulty, acknowledging God's faithfulness in carrying us through, and then we can refer back to it when we face the next struggle. Even when we don't understand and even when we don't have the answers to our questions, we can believe that God is faithful. Even though we cannot imagine where God is going to lead us or what our future is going to look like, we can have peace in knowing that God is in control. After we experienced years of heartache, pain, and loss, God blessed my husband and me with a precious little girl. I did not understand what God intended in His perfect plan for my life, but I learned that I can trust Him with all of my heart.

28

A Good Work in You

Leslie B. Vorndran

MY STORY

With one daughter at home and prayers for additional children, my husband and I walked out of the silent shame of infertility into the hope-filled world of reproductive therapy. Our first pregnancy had happened easily enough that we never expected to face several years of trying, only to have doctors confirm the heartbreak: we would be unable to conceive naturally again. In fact, our doctors weren't sure how we had been able to conceive our first child with the preexisting but previously undiagnosed medical conditions that both my husband and I had.

I was crushed and felt betrayed by my body's inability to do what I believed God had created it to do. Together with this husband of mine—whom God had given to me in perfect union—I would be unable to conceive. The promise of a child was replaced with insecurities about our compatibility, intimacy, and marriage. No amount of "You just need to relax" advice was going to fix this problem. Weekend getaways weren't quite the same for us. Sex is a wonderful thing in marriage, but prescribed sex every other day for months on end can lose its luster.

I was guilt-ridden for feeling devastated, as if I weren't thankful enough for the one gift we had been given. With the new truth facing us, we could have counted our daughter as our miracle and moved on to raising an only child, but we felt called to expand our family. We sought spiritual counsel about the controversies surrounding IVF. As Christians, this science-driven method of procreating raises questions, yet we believe that God's desire for us is life and relationships. If our family were to be blessed with another child, God would still be in control of the conception, no matter what method we used. And so we pursued IVF. To be honest, I was terrified and ready to quit before we began. If not for my husband's courage, my first visit to the infertility clinic would have been my last.

> If our family were to be blessed with another child, God would still be in control of the conception, no matter what method we used.

I watched with a mixture of curiosity and awkwardness as the doctor deftly drew a sketch of my ovaries and a timeline to get them in working order. To him, this was routine. To us, it was everything. In the months that followed, I obeyed the doctor's instructions precisely, injecting myself daily on schedule, enduring repeated blood tests and sonograms, and generally feeling like a science experiment. My body did cooperate, producing a large number of high-quality eggs that resulted in a fair number of living embryos. After the infamous two-week wait, we were elated to learn I was finally pregnant! Our first IVF cycle had been so successful that we were even able to cryopreserve two remaining embryos, two future babies.

Now two beautiful daughters filled our lives and hearts with joy. Was it selfish to desire another child? With two healthy children, each a miracle in her own right, how much more could we ask God and science to produce for us? Yet we greatly desired a larger family and had embryos waiting on ice. We spent months debating the pros and cons of trying again, something that—in a more typical scenario—can provide romantic intimacy for a couple. For us, we knew it meant a different type of closeness, a clinical intimacy: weeks of intramuscular shots, more tests, and the anxiety of thawing our embryo with hopes it would survive long enough to be implanted in my womb. And yet, if we didn't use our embryos, what would become of the babies created from my eggs and my husband's sperm? Our faith tells us these are babies, not bits of biological matter. What would God do with the souls of our children if we didn't try to carry them to term?

After many conversations and tears, my husband and I embraced the idea of bringing another baby into the world. And yet we didn't. My pregnancy—the baby we had fallen in love with, the promise of another child in our family—failed only a couple weeks in. I suppose I could count myself lucky to not lose a baby late in pregnancy. Except with me, and actually with anyone facing infertility, it's different. In order to submit myself to the pain and vulnerability of the IVF process, I had fully wrapped my mind and heart around this child. I had prepared to be pregnant months before the embryo would grow in my womb. Just as much as I loved my first two babies in utero, this child was mine. Then my child was gone. My pregnancy was nothing more than a statistic. Grief threatened to shatter both my husband and me. Yet, in God's goodness, He drew us closer to Himself and to one another, and one day in heaven we will praise God for this gift He gave us in that loss.

After a year, God gave us strength enough to transfer our last remaining embryo. With friends and loved ones praying for our frozen baby, we stepped out in faith. This time I felt God's presence as He pounded the shores of my heart with His words of affirmation. In the loss of our third pregnancy and the conception of our fourth child, God revealed His presence to me so clearly: there was no question He walked this path with us. First He strengthened our faith, our marriage, and our family, and then He breathed life into that last embryo and granted us the gift of a baby boy.

MY STRUGGLE

Jealousy, comparison, guilt, doubt—I was not an exemplary infertile woman, certainly not one whose faith in the Author of life shone forth brightly. Those years of pain and our longing—nine years between the birth of our first child and the birth of our last—now run through my memory like short verses of lamentations, but the daily struggle was long and trying. Above all, the biggest hurdle for me was the silence of it all. The medical side of IVF doesn't offer time for long deliberations and, even worse, few venues for discussion. Our desire for and our inability to have children were always on my mind, yet those matters were not considered appropriate to be on my lips. We felt awkward sharing this great burden even among our dearest friends, many of whom were expanding their own families.

> God revealed His presence to me so clearly: there
> was no question He walked this path with us.

When fertility treatments were first prescribed, I didn't know where to start. I reached out to the only woman I knew who had undergone IVF treatments. We barely knew one another, but she was happy to support another woman facing infertility. Whenever I felt alone, struggled to process the many questions and emotions, or was prompted to cry over another friend's pregnancy announcement, I called on her. Throughout the years of treatments and secrets shared, she has become one of my closest friends. It was to her I could admit envy and anger when I was too embarrassed to bring my weakness directly to God. Our Father's greatest desire for us is to have a relationship with Him. Sometimes He uses friendships to draw us closer to Himself even when we think He is absent from our daily struggles.

MY STRENGTH

It wasn't until the loss of our third pregnancy that I began to find community in our pain. After my tears were spent, I reached out through the most natural outlet I know—writing. The words came as easily as the tears had. With my husband's blessing, I shared with the blogosphere our most intimate and painful experiences, not knowing what would become of it. God, in His infinite goodness, turned my simple offering into blessings for us and for others.

Friends came forward to share their own experiences of loss and longing, to connect with others in their own pain, to pray over us, and to give us opportunities to share our story so that it might encourage others. When the time came to attempt our final round of IVF, rather than find ourselves lost in silent shame, we were surrounded by an army of prayer warriors. We believed from the start—and still believe—that God's desire for us is life and relationships: He encouraged our vulnerability, and He gave us the gift of deeper friendships and a stronger faith community.

MY SCRIPTURE

> *He who has begun a good work in you will complete*
> *it until the day of Jesus Christ (Philippians 1:6).*

The journey my family traveled for our children was full of heartbreak and waiting. To say I developed patience would paint me in a better light than I deserve. I cried, begged, and whined to God on a regular basis. I questioned Him, asked guidance of others, and worried selfishly. Shamefully, I did not hold fast to any one promise of Scripture. I lost my hope several times, but I never let go of the truth of God's ultimate goodness. We are not here for a life of ease, but to be refined, to grow, to be used for His glory, to love, and to be loved. I pray God's record of my heart will find, laced in the threads of my suffering, faithful prayers for His promises to be known in and through me.

29

Wait for It

Stefanie Vourron

MY STORY

When I began menstruating as a young girl, I thought it was terrible. I bled heavily and would miss school on occasion. My mother finally took me to a gynecologist to see if my heavy bleeding was abnormal. Ultimately, an ultrasound revealed I had a bicornuate uterus, which in my case means that it's shaped like a heart and really did not present any major medical problems, just discomfort.

Fast-forward ten years. I was a 21-year-old college student when I started to have terrible pains in my stomach. I made an appointment with my gynecologist. After doing an ultrasound, he informed me that I would be admitted to the hospital the next day to have two grapefruit-sized tumors removed from my ovaries and uterus. When I woke up after the surgery with 21 metal staples from my belly button to my pubic bone, I was told I still had my uterus but not much of my ovaries. The good news was that the tumors were benign and removed. The bad news was that the condition of my ovaries would make it difficult for me to have children. This information was life changing. Although at this point in my life I had never really thought about having children, now I felt as though I had no choice.

For most of my twenties, I convinced myself that I never wanted to get married or have a family anyway. I surrounded myself with single, childless people. In hindsight, it was a way of protecting myself from relationships that could end due to the possibility I would not be able to have children. I had finished college and landed a great job, but I was not fulfilled.

In my late twenties I began asking God to bring a man into my life who loved God and who came from a stable family. That was important to me due to my parents' divorce. Growing up, I had no positive marital role models. My father was married three times, and my mom remained single.

> For most of my twenties, I convinced myself that
> I never wanted to get married or have a family
> anyway...It was a way of protecting myself.

God answered my prayers three years later when I crossed paths with a middle-school friend on a holiday weekend. We were suddenly smitten with each other and started dating immediately. I told him early on that I might not be able to have children, and he told me it didn't matter because there were other options we could pursue.

After a couple years of marriage, we were not getting pregnant. We enjoyed our married life with exciting travels and working on a private yacht together, but not getting pregnant and not knowing if it was a possibility loomed over us. We decided to see a fertility specialist.

After our first consultation, the doctor reviewed our medical history. He concluded that I should find a surrogate to carry a baby for me and that I should also find an egg donor so we could have healthy, viable eggs. I was crushed. The news was as damaging as it was when I had my surgery many years before. I decided to get a second opinion.

When I met the next doctor, I told him I would like nothing more than to carry a child and experience pregnancy. He did many tests and decided that without giving me medications to begin ovulation, he would not know about my egg reserve. He did not find anything wrong with my uterus except that it was not ideally shaped. We did two rounds of trying to get my ovaries to produce eggs without any results. The doctor concluded that because of my surgery, my ovaries were not going to produce any eggs. This news was devastating. Even though I had been told this might happen, I was not ready for the reality. I prayed for acceptance and peace.

My doctor told me of a donor egg program for women who did not produce their own eggs. He believed that my uterus could carry a child, but I would need donor eggs to mix with my husband's sperm to create embryos. I thought this was the craziest thing I had ever heard, but I was hopeful and excited.

We found a suitable donor and ended up with 15 embryos. The first, second, third, and fourth transfers did not result in pregnancy. We eventually got pregnant twice but miscarried both times. After the second miscarriage, I told my doctor I didn't want to try anymore. He explained once again that my uterus was perfect for carrying a child and that I already had the medication to do another round, so what did I have to lose? My doctor knew exactly what to say because our money was evaporating.

My husband and I decided to do one more round to finish off the medication we had already purchased. When I was two months shy of turning 39, our seventh transfer resulted in our healthy, happy, busy boy. Every time he says, "Mom," my heart pitter-patters.

MY STRUGGLE

During my 20-year impersonation of a woman who did not want children, I fooled everyone into believing this was who I was. I even fooled myself. My girlfriends were afraid to tell me they were getting married or going to have a child, nervous that I might criticize them. I hid behind my job, schooling, and career in an effort to stay busy and not be involved with married couples and families.

When my husband and I started dating, we knew we were going to get married. It was the first time I ever envisioned myself as a wife. My husband told several of his friends after our first date that I was the girl he was going to marry. I called my mom and told her I had met my husband. She was flabbergasted, to say the least, since she had never heard me discuss marriage before. As suddenly as I fell in love with my husband, I fell in love with the idea of having a child. I wanted those two things more than ever!

MY STRENGTH

Infertility treatment is no easy task with all the doctor appointments, paperwork, blood work, medications, specimen collections, and financial hardships. My strength came from the people around me. My amazing husband endured my ups and downs while I was on some hefty hormones for four years. He comforted me, cried with me, and reminded me that this was his journey too.

My mother accompanied me to countless doctor visits that were almost an hour's drive away. She encouraged me to keep moving forward in my pursuit to have a baby because she pictured me as a mother. When I complained about the amount of money my husband and I were spending with no positive outcome, she encouraged me to keep going, saying that I would never look back on the money we spent once we had a child. She was 100 percent correct.

My mother-in-law put a note in the Western Wall on a trip to Israel. The paper had my name and my husband's name, and she prayed that God would give us a child. My father-in-law took pictures of her doing this, and she gave them to me on the day of my son's birth, three years after that trip.

My doctor gave me strength and hope when I had none left by, for instance, simply calling me after a procedure to see how I was doing. He also gave me the confidence that I could carry a child, which was comforting coming from a professional after I had only heard for so many years how hard it would be.

MY SCRIPTURE

> *Write the vision*
> *And make it plain on tablets,*
> *That he may run who reads it.*
> *For the vision is yet for an appointed time;*
> *But at the end it will speak, and it will not lie.*
> *Though it tarries, wait for it;*
> *Because it will surely come,*
> *It will not tarry (Habakkuk 2:2-3).*

My mother-in-law wrote this scripture on an index card for me during the first years of my struggle. I originally put it on my bathroom mirror, then moved it to the dashboard in my car, and finally wrote it on five index cards and put them in various places. These verses gave me strength. The words *appointed time* still jump out at me. I knew I wouldn't have a child at the time I appointed, my husband appointed, or my doctor appointed. I did not always like this reality, but I chose to accept it. I knew that having a baby was bigger than me and that I was not in control. I knew deep in my heart that a baby would be given to us in God's time.

Early on in my infertility struggle, I turned to God and prayed continually that He would give us a child someway, somehow. I thank God for our precious miracle every day. I also thank God for keeping our marriage together and strengthening it. I live each day to the fullest and do not take one second for granted. I praise God for my amazing life, and I would not trade any part of my journey.

30

Father of Compassion

Kathe Wunnenberg

MY STORY

I'm from a family of fertility-challenged women. My grannie and great-grandmother longed for and lost children through miscarriage, stillbirth, and early infant death. Even my mother suffered from secondary infertility after the birth of my older brother. When she finally conceived, she miscarried early in her pregnancy. She endured her loss in silence. Most people from her generation did not share openly about pregnancy or fertility challenges. My mom did not give up but became more determined to have a second child. She journeyed frequently to see a doctor many miles away from her rural town. Monthly disappointments did not stop her. Her perseverance finally paid off when my older brother was six. The seed of faith and hope God planted in her heart finally blossomed into a child: ME! Because of my mom and the women in my family before her, who had also longed for children and persevered, you are reading this story from me.

Like the women in my family who have gone before me, conceiving a child did not come easily for me. I married my college sweetheart after graduation and passionately pursued a career for the first few years of our marriage. I wasn't convinced motherhood was for me. I believed Satan's lie that I would not be a good mom because of my parents' divorce when I was a child. My husband desperately wanted a family of his own after losing both of his parents as a young boy. He was patient, and he prayed.

When God finally answered my husband's prayer and changed my heart, I was in my late twenties. I assumed I would get pregnant easily like most of my friends and then add "motherhood" to my life resumé. To my frustration, getting pregnant didn't happen as I planned. Instead, I started an unexpected journey through infertility. Temperature charts, ovulation tests, and doctor visits became part of my regular routine. When I finally did conceive and shared the news, I miscarried our first child a few days later. I was disappointed but didn't feel deeply about the loss of our child at that time.

Unaware that my pain was hidden and would resurface later in my life, I pressed on. In spite of my doctor's hope for me to conceive again quickly, I didn't, and he had no explanation why. Both my husband and I felt God prompting us to adopt, so we started the process while trying to also conceive. Adoption had been part of my plans since I was seven and a neighbor from a nearby farm entrusted me with a newborn orphaned baby goat to raise. I enthusiastically embraced my new role and the responsibilities of round-the-clock bottle feeding. I bonded quickly and referred to Puddles the goat as "my first kid." I grieved deeply when I had to return him to the farm several months later. From that time on I boasted, "Someday I'm going to adopt a baby." About two years after beginning the process with a Christian adoption agency, God filled our hearts with joy and our arms with our infant son, Jake.

I'm still amazed at how God planted the seed of adoption in my heart long ago through my childhood experience of raising a goat, a seed that eventually grew into a longing for a child who would be grafted into our family. When our son became a toddler, he began to pray for "a baby to grow in Mommy's belly." I was shocked, but he persisted. A couple of years later, the doctor announced, "You're pregnant!" We celebrated God's answer to prayer. However, our short-lived joy turned into sorrow when we discovered on Good Friday that our unborn son had anencephaly, a fatal birth defect. I found myself in my own Garden of Gethsemane crying out, "God, please take this cup of suffering from me!" By Easter morning, I had released my anguish and my unborn son into His care when I prayed, "Not my will but Thine be done."

During the long months waiting for the birth of our son, I was encouraged by the stories of other women who had endured similar pain. I was determined to praise God no matter the outcome. On August 22, John Samuel was born, and within a few hours he entered God's eternal presence. His brief life changed mine forever. Although my arms were empty when I left the hospital, my heart was filled with an urgent desire for God to enlarge my life through loss and transform my hurt into hope to help others. I wasn't expecting *more* losses.

> I released my anguish and my unborn son into His care when I prayed, "Not my will but Thine be done."

During the next year, I lost two more babies through miscarriage. When the doctor confirmed I was pregnant with a fifth child, I was terrified at the thought of another loss. I was 40. Again, God brought to my mind the faithful women from my family who had faced similar challenges and endured. With renewed courage and faith, I pressed on.

After nearly two decades of marriage, four babies in heaven, and a nine-year-old adopted son, I finally crossed over to birth a *living* son, Joshua. Ironically, my first devotional book, *Grieving the Loss of a Loved One*, was also released around the same time. Two years later, at age 42, I birthed another healthy son, Jordan, and amazingly, my second devotional book, *Grieving the Child I Never Knew*, was also released. My family was complete. Although no more babies were born, more books were released, and I also started an organization dedicated to mentoring women and multiplying hope. Looking back now through my life, I see how infertility and loss have enlarged me and increased my compassion for others. I also see God's plan and His purpose for my pain.

MY STRUGGLE

I've learned that infertility is a private and personal pain. While many choose to suffer in silence, I struggled to be silent and chose to speak up. At times, I'm sure I made others feel uncomfortable with the topics I discussed. I also struggled with feeling alone or misunderstood by others when I shared openly about fertility challenges.

> I see how infertility and loss have enlarged me
> and increased my compassion for others.

Because I understand the hidden hurt behind holidays, baby showers, and Mother's Day, I became a proactive communicator and challenged church leaders—and anyone who would listen—to also recognize in their Mother's Day celebrations women who longed for or had lost children. Sometimes I struggled to forgive people who ignored or minimized my pain or who did or said hurtful things. I prayed Jesus's words often: "Father, forgive them because they don't know what they're doing."

MY STRENGTH

I found strength and comfort in God's Word, prayer, the Holy Spirit, and the lives of other women. When I read God's Word daily, I expected Him to speak to me. Throughout my infertility journey, I highlighted or underlined scriptures in my Bible and wrote my name or another person's in specific verses, making them a prayer for myself or for others. I also journaled. I recorded thoughts, feelings, ideas, prayers, and insights from God's Word.

I invited the Holy Spirit to be my Comforter (John 14:26 KJV) and to empower me (Ephesians 3:20). When I cried out in times of sorrow or uncertainty, He might respond by leading me to a timely scripture, song, or idea that gave me hope. Other times He led me to a beautiful outdoor setting and refreshed me with His creation. Often, He brought other similarly challenged women to mind who understood my struggles, women like my mom, grannie, and great-grandmother. The lives and stories of Sarah, Hannah, and Elizabeth from the Bible strengthened me then and now. Connecting with other women online, by text, face-to-face, at one of my small-group retreats, or on my annual "Mothers Who Have Lost Children" bus trips brought comfort and hope to me.

When I asked God to enlarge my life through my longing and loss, and to transform my hurt into hope to help others, He did. He empowered me to write and speak my story to strengthen other women and to encourage them to do the same.

MY SCRIPTURE

> *Praise be to the God and Father of our Lord Jesus Christ, the Father of compassion and the God of all comfort, who comforts us in all our troubles, so that we can comfort those in any trouble with the comfort we ourselves receive from God (2 Corinthians 1:3-4 NIV).*

My personal motto, the signature phrase I share often, and the wisdom I live by is "We go through what we go through, to help others go through what we went through." Those who know me well or have attended my retreats, workshops, or bus trips can probably recite it too. It is inspired by Paul's words in 2 Corinthians 1:3-4, truth that encouraged me to receive comfort during my many times of suffering. The two words *so that* gave purpose to my pain. I needed to receive comfort in all my troubles, *so that* I can give God's comfort to others.

Meet Our Contributors

The women who are featured on the pages of this book shared their deeply personal stories for the purpose of giving hope to others who are experiencing infertility. Even though they may never meet you, they are honored to journey beside you with their words.

Katherine Alumbaugh lives in the Bay Area of California with her husband and daughter. She gave up gluten for a while during infertility treatment and has now taken up bread making to make up for lost time and calories. When not chasing her daughter in the California sunshine, she loves to cook, read, and write. She blogs at www.kalumbaugh.com.

Meghann Bowman is wife to an awesome guy, a retired attorney, and a mother to a train- and truck-loving little boy and a baby girl. She enjoys outdoor time and snuggling with her family. Together, they reside in the Washington, DC metro area.

Jillian Burden lives in Michigan with her husband, John. Together they have three little boys through international adoption and embryo adoption. A seminary graduate, Jillian loves talking and writing about faith and spirituality. You can find her on Instagram @jillian_burden.

Valorie Burton is the founder of The Coaching and Positive Psychology (CAPP) Institute and serves as a certified personal and executive coach, helping people get unstuck and be unstoppable in every area of life. She is a national speaker and bestselling author of 12 books, including *Successful Women Think Differently* and *Where Will You Go from Here?* She has written for numerous publications, including *Essence, Woman's Day,* and *O, The Oprah Magazine.* She has appeared on the Today Show, the Dr. Oz Show, CNN, and HLN. Get her free guided meditations at www.valorieburton.com. https://www.facebook.com/valorieburton.

Karen DeVries's baby-wonders are grown up, but still hold the same baby-love in her heart. She and her husband, Dale, have transitioned from a family home with a child-friendly yard to an age-appropriate condo where the driveway and front walk are magically shoveled on snowy days. She will never outgrow her love of roller coasters or curling up with a book and bold cup of hazelnut coffee. Karen works in early childhood education, which allows her to play golf during summer break and sled with her young students in the winter. In all seasons she wants to keep childlike faith, hope, and perspective.

Shelby Doll was born and raised in West Michigan, where she resides with her handsome husband, spunky little girl, precious little guy, and crazy dog. She is a daughter of God, stay-at-home mom, and host mom for Safe Families for Children, and an active member of her church. She loves spending time with her family, being a part-time chicken farmer, and going on adventures. shelbydoll1196@gmail.com

Donna Fagerstrom is an identical twin and was born in Holland, Michigan, where she accepted Christ at the age of six. She has worked in a variety of Christian leadership and support roles and is committed to praying for church leaders. She is an encourager, worshipper, speaker, writer, and author of *Every Mourning,* a daily devotional for people in grief. In 2010 Donna received "The Woman of Influence" award from Cornerstone University. She misses living near her daughter, son-in-love, and two precious granddaughters, but is quick to say, "There is joy in serving Jesus and others."

Karen Granger is a career public relations professional working in both business and ministry sectors. Her joy in being a Hallmark Channel-loving, *Downton Abbey*-drama fan is often squelched in a home where soccer, clay-shooting, camping, and masculine video games rule. She spent years as a local Chamber of Commerce CEO and can tell you about all the best restaurants and businesses in Delray Beach, Florida. Currently Karen works as an advocate for children in foster care with 4KIDS of South Florida. When the Grangers are not at home in the South, they love spending time with friends and family in states that begin with M—Maryland, Maine, and Montana.

Amanda Hope Haley has a Master of Theological Studies in Hebrew Scripture and Interpretation from Harvard University. She contributed to *The Voice* Bible as a translator, writer, and editor, and she has been a content editor and ghostwriter for popular Christian authors. Amanda maintains the blog *Healthy and Hopeful,* where she encourages women to live whole lives in community with God, family, and each other. Her first book, *Barren Among the Fruitful: Navigating Infertility with Hope, Wisdom, and Patience*, was released by HarperCollins Christian Publishers in 2014. Amanda and her husband, David, recently moved from Denver to Chattanooga, Tennessee, where they are enjoying new friends and new adventures while raising their basset hound, Copper. You may reach Amanda and learn about her next book with Harvest House Publishers through her website: www.amandahopehaley.com.

Mary Hassinger has had many jobs over the years, but things usually led back to the theme of KIDS. She's been a middle-school classroom teacher, a Sunday school teacher, an adult literacy coordinator, and is currently a senior editor at a publisher of Christian children's products. Mary loves spending time with her big, loud, still-naughty five brothers, their families, and her sidekick, Maggie (a.k.a. her daughter).

MacKenzie Clark Howard and her husband, Josh, live in the country in Tennessee with their son and two dogs. They are next door to her parents and down the lane from her brother and his family. Her family is her treasure, and she cherishes this gift. The Howards have an embarrassingly large collection of Starbucks mugs. MacKenzie loves a hot coconut milk chai tea latte, and Josh enjoys a variety of iced coffees. They realized they had passed their problem on to the next generation one morning when their four-year-old said, "Hey, guys! I've got a good idea. Let's go to Starbucks for some breakfast sandwiches." Josh and MacKenzie are passionate about adoption and would love to connect with you. If you'd like to know more about adoption or have someone pray with you, please reach out to them at mackenzieclarkhoward@gmail.com.

Sara M. Howard treasures the roles of being a wife and a mother through adoption. She is an author, speaker, registered nurse, and life coach focusing on health and wellness. She loves to encourage others to find the hope and the joy in life that God wants them to have. Sara thrives on staying busy with five spirited and active children. You might occasionally find her sneaking off to get a sip of ice-cold, fizzing Coca-Cola since she is convinced it might be a little taste of heaven. www.EncourageHope.com

Darci Irwin is currently a stay-at-home mama to two daughters, Kyra Saige and Arlie Mave. Previously she worked in two different churches, a university, and a nonprofit organization supporting orphans around the world. She obtained an undergraduate degree in psychology and a master's degree in management. She enjoys helping people become the best versions of themselves they can be through acts of courage. For psychology junkies, she's an ENFJ and a 3w2. She loves raspberries, snail mail, hot yoga, travel, reading, almond milk lattes, decorating, decluttering, easy new recipes, macaroons, Chatbooks, fuzzy socks, color, epic family dance parties, and creating margin for the good stuff of life.

Wendi Kitsteiner is a former city girl now living on a farm in the middle of nowhere, Tennessee, with her husband and four young children who came through her own and another mother's womb. She is passionate about the causes of infertility, adoption, and keeping it real as a mom—which means if you visit her, expect chocolate and chaos. You can follow her at flakymn.blogspot.com or becauseofisaac.org.

Ke-Jia Liu was born in Beijing, China, and moved to Michigan with her family when she was nine. She currently lives in Southern California with her husband and her two kids. Ke-Jia works as an optometrist, and in her spare time she enjoys baking, shopping, decorating, and spending time at the beach with her family.

Zena Dell Lowe is a writer, director, and producer at Mission Ranch Films—and a recently published comic book writer. She has worked professionally in the entertainment industry for over 15 years. She teaches advanced classes on writing at numerous writers' conferences across the country and as an adjunct professor at Covenant College in Lookout Mountain, Georgia, and Regent University in Virginia Beach, Virginia. Zena currently resides in Bozeman, Montana, where she enjoys floating down the Madison River with friends in the summer, attending the sporting events of her nieces and nephews in the winter, and playing fetch with her sweet pup, Lulu, all year long. To find out more about Zena, check out her website at www.missionranchfilms.com or find her on Vimeo at https://vimeo.com/user40111715/videos.

Kelly Miller is a wife, mother of Sloane and baby Reese, and a secondary school counselor. She loves all things Texas Rangers, Dallas Cowboys, and Texas A&M Aggies. She was born way up in the north but made her way to Texas as fast as she could. She is also devoted to teaching the Word of God, equipping women for ministry, and bringing awareness to the struggle of infertility. kellyt18@gmail.com

Katie Norris serves as CEO and film producer for Fotolanthropy, a nonprofit film organization that celebrates hope-giving stories of people who have defied great odds. She is the producer of the award-winning feature documentaries *Travis: A Soldier's Story* and *The Luckiest Man*. To help fund Fotolanthropy's work, Katie also founded FOTO, an American-made brand of genuine leather products, most notably the Fotostrap. Katie frequently speaks about her journey as an entrepreneur and her journey with infertility, but she is most thankful to serve as mom to her daughter, Rose. She resides in Dallas, Texas, with her family and adventures as often as possible to the mountains in Colorado. Email: katie@katienorris.net and Instagram: @katienorrisfoto

Megan O'Connell is an educator turned stay-at-home mommy. She married her 6'8" college sweetheart, who towers over her petite self, and together they try to keep up with their silly and vivacious little boy. Megan is driven by real relationships where people support and encourage one another by being transparent about the yuck along with the fun. You can find her at Mothering the Toddling, where she blogs about building community, secondary infertility, and motherhood shenanigans. Blog website: www.motheringthetoddling.com

Grace O'Connor lives with her husband and three boys in a house full of trucks, homemade obstacle courses, and wrestling matches. While she and her husband work outside of the home, they both have part-time jobs filling snack requests from their children.

Becky Schrotenboer is mom to three awesome kiddos from Colombia. She's an interior designer by trade, but in her spare time she loves to run, read, and hang out with her husband and kids. Her family calls Grand Rapids, Michigan, home, and they love to spend time playing games in the yard and on the water at their "Up North" cottage. She says, "I hope you are blessed by this book as I have been blessed by the wonderful world of adoption!"

Shay Shull is a cookbook author, lifestyle blogger, travel agency owner, wife, and mama who loves making every day special for her family. She likes to spend time with girlfriends, watch Red Sox baseball, drink an insane amount of coffee, read her Bible, and make a yummy dinner each night. She is passionate about traveling, adoption, food, and especially Jesus. You can connect with Shay at www.http://mixandmatchmama.com.

Katie Cruice Smith is a freelance writer and editor—and the joyful mother of three crazy kids. When she isn't correcting someone else's grammar, she's busy sharing her own kids' questions in her new children's book *Why Did You Choose Me?* Katie is an expert at cleaning up spilled milk, stepping on Legos, kissing boo-boos, and tackling supper for picky eaters. You can laugh, groan, and cry with her as you read her everyday misadventures in motherhood at www.katiecruicesmith.com. Or follow her on Facebook at Katie Cruice Smith, Author; on Twitter @authorktcsmith; or on Instagram @authorkatiesmith.

Melissa Sodoma lives in South Florida where she is a stay-at-home mom to her five children. For the last ten years, she has been in leadership at her local MOPS (Mothers of Preschoolers) group. She is working on her psychology degree to become a licensed mental health counselor. Melissa also stays busy with Sodoma Farms, the little self-proclaimed family business that is actually more of a fun family project. Together, they take care of their 15 fruit trees and nine chickens, make jams, and sell fresh eggs and fruit to their neighbors. You can reach her at Melissa_sodoma@yahoo.com.

Stephanie Tait is a blogger, author, and speaker. Her mix of quick-witted humor and a no-holds-barred style of authentic sharing makes for a truly unique voice, one that draws a community of readers longing for something refreshingly raw yet still anchored in hope. She lives in Salem, Oregon, with her loyal Canadian husband, Bobby, and her miracle boys, Aidan and Jack. If you're ever in Salem, you'll probably find her grabbing a cold brew at Dutch Bros Coffee, getting into trouble with her husband later at Target, or gathering supplies for her latest DIY project at Hobby Lobby or Lowe's. Blog: www.thejoyparadeblog.com Facebook: /stephanie tait; Twitter: @joyparadeblog; Instagram: @thejoyparade; Email: thejoy parade@gmail.com

LaShea Udoaka is an educator, proud Air Force wife, mother, and sister in Christ. She is currently a math teacher at an American high school in Germany and is active in the women's ministry at her church. LaShea enjoys reading, event planning, and encouraging women through God's Word. She has a special place in her heart for African-American adoption and transracial adoptions of African-American children. LaShea believes that adoption is a spiritual journey and connects for a lifetime everyone who is involved. To reach LaShea, please contact her via Facebook Messenger (profile name: LaShea Udoaka).

Joan Van Wyck was born in Potchefstroom, South Africa, and moved to Sheboygan, Wisconsin, with her family when she was four years old. After graduating from Calvin College in Grand Rapids, Michigan, she and her husband moved to Florida. She has many interests including photography, waterskiing, and playing the piano. She has traveled all over the world and has had the opportunity to pose for a picture in front of her childhood home in South Africa. Joan is a wife, mother, and grandmother, and she is active in church ministry.

Leslie B. Vorndran is wife to a really great guy and mother to two daughters and a son. She continually seeks to find joy in the everyday, in the extraordinary, and in the mundane. In her spare time, she is a leader of her local MOPS group and participates in as many mission trips as she can.

Stefanie Vourron feels fortunate to live on an island near Palm Beach, Florida. She always has sand in her car, dryer, and house because she cannot escape it. While her husband and son love to do anything on the water, she prefers watching them from shore. She is a lifelong gym enthusiast and may break out in dance anywhere. She loves telling personal stories and will often do something crazy just to have a good story to tell. She has been teaching fitness classes for several years and also works in property management and real estate—all of which give her many storytelling opportunities.

Kathe Wunnenberg is a hopelifter who believes God can transform anything you offer Him into hope you can use to help others. As a mom who has experienced three miscarriages and the death of an infant, Kathe understands the pain of infertility and loss. Her speaking and her books—*Grieving the Loss of a Loved One, Grieving the Child I Never Knew, Longing for a Child,* and *Hopelifter: Creative Ways to Spread Hope When Life Hurts*—have impacted multitudes. She is the founder and president of Hopelifters Unlimited, a mentoring, training, and resource organization. She lives in Phoenix, Arizona, with her husband. They have three living sons and four sons in heaven. Connect with her at www.hopelifters.com; Facebook: hopeliftersunlimited; Twitter: @hopelifters.

Acknowledgments

We are truly grateful to those who went the extra mile to help us make this book a reality:

To Kathleen Kerr and the Harvest House team: Sherrie Slopianka, Betty Fletcher, Hope Lyda, Jessica Ballestrazze, Karri James, Kyler Dougherty, Heather Decker, Christianne Debysingh, Shelby Zacharias, and Jody Lyon.

A special thanks also to Elisa Morgan, Jennifer Saake, Wendy Kitsteiner, Karen DeVries, Karen Neumair, Teri McKinley, and Scott Bowman.

To learn more about Harvest House books and
to read sample chapters, log on to our website:
www.harvesthousepublishers.com

HARVEST HOUSE PUBLISHERS
EUGENE, OREGON